ALL ABOUT
PIES & TARTS

ALL ABOUT
PIES & TARTS

IRMA S. ROMBAUER
MARION ROMBAUER BECKER
ETHAN BECKER

PHOTOGRAPHY BY TUCKER & HOSSLER

SCRIBNER

NEW YORK • LONDON • TORONTO • SYDNEY • SINGAPORE

SCRIBNER
1230 Avenue of the Americas
New York, NY 10020

WELDON OWEN INC.
Chief Executive Officer: John Owen
President: Terry Newell
Chief Operating Officer: Larry Partington
Vice President, International Sales: Stuart Laurence
Publisher: Roger Shaw
Creative Director: Gaye Allen
Associate Publisher: Val Cipollone
Senior Editor: Sarah Lemas
Associate Editor: Anna Mantzaris
Consulting Editor: Barbara Ottenhoff
Art Director: Ramsey Rickart
Designer: Sarah Gifford
Photo Editor: Lisa Lee
Production Manager: Chris Hemesath
Shipping and Production Coordinator: Libby Temple
Production: Joan Olson
Food Stylist: Dan Becker
Assistant Food Stylist: Leslie Busch
Step-by-Step Photographer: Mike Falconer
Step-by-Step Food Stylist: Andrea Lucich

Joy of Cooking All About series was designed
and produced by Weldon Owen Inc.,
814 Montgomery Street, San Francisco,
California 94133

Set in Joanna MT and Gill Sans

Separations by Bright Arts Singapore
Printed in Singapore by Tien Wah Press (Pte.) Ltd.

10 9 8 7 6 5 4 3 2 1

Library of Congress Cataloging-in-Publication Data
Rombauer, Irma von Starkloff, 1877-1962.
  Joy of cooking. All about pies & tarts/Irma S. Rombauer,
Marion Rombauer Becker, Ethan Becker.
  p. cm — (Joy of cooking all about series)
  Includes index.
  ISBN 0-7432-2518-X
  1. Pies. I. Title: All about pies & tarts. II. Becker,
Marion Rombauer. III. Becker, Ethan. IV. Title. V. Series.
TX773 .R65 2002
641.8'652—dc21
                                    2002019520

Recipe shown on half-title page: Cherry Pie, 43
Recipes shown on title page: Half-Covered Berry
or Peach Galette and Yeasted French Galette, 71

CONTENTS

FOREWORD

The world offers us a profusion of pies, from Cornish pasties to Mexican tamales, French tarts to German strudels. And we have the good luck that they all have made their way to the United States. Our love of pies is almost a tenet of our patritotism.

My own love of pies led me to boycott cheesecake long ago, which in my view, usurps too much space on menus. At our table we continue to enjoy the same kinds of pies Granny Rom and Mom used to bake: peach custard, pecan, banana cream, and lemon meringue, my childhood favorite.

Pies are too good not to eat more often—whether savory Greek spanikopita or American apple pie. As you glance through these pages, we are certain that temptation will win and you will be headed kitchenward.

This collection of kitchen-tested recipes is adapted from the latest edition of the Joy of Cooking. Just as our family has done for generations, we have worked to make this version of JOY a little bit better than the last. As a result, you'll find that some notes, recipes, and techniques have been changed to improve their clarity and usefulness. Since 1931, the Joy of Cooking has constantly evolved. And now, the All About series has taken JOY to a whole new stage, as you will see from the beautiful color photographs of finished treats and clearly illustrated instructions for preparing and enjoying them. Granny Rom and Mom would have been delighted.

I'm sure you'll find All About Pies & Tarts to be both a useful and an enduring companion in your kitchen.

Enjoy!

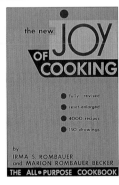

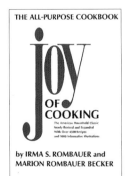

Ethan Becker pictured with his grandmother, Irma von Starkloff Rombauer (left), and his mother, Marion Rombauer Becker (right). Irma Rombauer published the first Joy of Cooking *at her own expense in 1931. Marion Rombauer Becker became coauthor in 1951.* JOY *as it has progressed through the decades (from top left to bottom right): the 1931 edition with Marion's depiction of St. Martha of Bethany, said to be the patron saint of cooking, "slaying the dragon of kitchen drudgery"; the 1943 edition; the 1951 edition; the 1962 edition; the 1975 edition; and the 1997 edition.*

About Pies & Tarts

Pies came to America with the Pilgrims, and our love affair with these desserts has continued ever since. Southerners dote on pecan, chess, and sweet potato pies, New Englanders adore pumpkin pie, and the Pennsylvania Dutch never need an excuse to make shoofly pie. But pie-making has kept pace with changing times as well. In the last century, refrigeration made possible cream and chiffon pies, and now pies are filled with chocolate (lots of it), peanut butter, caramel, coffee, ice cream, or any mousse imaginable. Though still based on traditional recipes, contemporary fruit pies contain more fruit and less sugar.

We used to think of tarts as small pies; they were usually open, and meant for individual servings. Today we call these tartlets, reserving the name tart for large pastries baked in tart pans and then unmolded before serving. While pie and tart methods overlap and crusts and fillings are often interchangeable, American tarts display a distinctly French style. Just as a French sandwich puts as much emphasis on the bread as it does on the filling, a French tart balances a small amount of filling with a superb crust. The wide, shallow tart shell provides an elegant base for arranging the fruit.

Some of the very same flaky, unsweetened crusts used to make dessert tarts do double duty as the bases for savory tarts. Choose a light, custard filling studded with bacon for a satisfying quiche, or opt for thinly sliced tomatoes, cheese, and herbs for a summertime treat. Not only can you play around with fillings, but you can also serve savory tarts in a number of ways: Cut bite-size pieces to present as hors d'oeuvres, or pair large wedges with a salad of mixed greens for an elegant lunch.

While savory tarts have bottom crusts, savory pies are either completely encased in pastry—such as Latin American empanadas, Italian pizza rustica, and English pasties— or covered just on top by a golden crust—such as American pot pies. In both cases, the pastry protects the meat or vegetable stuffing by locking in moisture. It also provides a crisp counterpart to the warm, flavorful filling.

So just as you'll find classic, covered sweet pies in these pages, so too will you encounter their savory equivalents, which likewise hearken back to America's beginnings.

Equipment for Pies and Tarts

There are two kinds of rolling pins—the American pin with handles, and the European pole. If you have never rolled out crust before, choose an American pin of a size and weight you find comfortable. European rolling pins are made either thick and uniformly cylindrical or slender and tapered at the ends. Once you get the hang of rolling out dough, you will want a tapered pin for the way it allows you to maneuver the dough to any effect, but many beginners find this one awkward to work with. Wood is the perfect material for all rolling pins.

Marble pins also work well. Hollow metal pins filled with ice water sweat; glass pins are beautiful to behold but fragile.

A pastry blender, a tool consisting of five or six bowed metal blades for blending flour and fat in flaky pastry, is essential. Also useful are a ruler to measure the thickness and width of the dough, a fluted pastry wheel (pastry jagger) for cutting decorative lattices, and a metal dough scraper. For weighting unfilled "blind-baked" crusts, metal pie weights are a good alternative to raw beans or rice, which burn and grow musty with

use. Some home bakers cover the edge of a pie with a shield to prevent overbrowning, but this has limited effect; the same benefit can be achieved with a ring cut from heavy aluminum foil.

American pie pans come in two standard diameters, 9 inches and 10 inches; the former has a capacity of around 4½ cups, and the latter, 6 cups. Glass pie pans produce wonderfully brown, crisp crusts, and they also let you check on the progress of the crust during baking, but heavy metal pans, whether matte, shiny, or black finish, are

perfectly acceptable. Do not use deep-dish glass pie pans for an ordinary pie, because they lack the flared rim needed to form the edge of the crust. Also avoid the flimsy nonstick metal pans often sold in supermarkets; they are too shallow to hold a standard amount of pie filling.

We wish some enterprising manufacturer would design tart pans that correlate precisely in capacity with standard American pie pans. Until that day comes, use a tart pan measuring 9½ or 10 inches across and 1 to 1¼ inches deep for 4 to 4½ cups filling, and a tart pan 11 inches in diameter and about 1 inch deep for 4½ to 6 cups filling. If you unmold a tart for serving, the pan must be a two-piece construction with a removable bottom. All two-piece tart pans are metal. Black-finish tart pans may produce slightly browner crusts, but crusts are less likely to stick in shiny metal pans.

Tartlet pans come in a great number of sizes, from 1½-inch miniature pans used to make hors d'oeuvre cases to 4½-inch pans for individual tartlets. They may be of one-piece or two-piece construction; they may have straight or sloping sides, and their sides may be either smooth or fluted. They are made in virtually every shape imaginable. Speaking broadly, buy wider shallow tartlet pans, as crusts tend to lose their shape during baking when formed in deep, narrow pans. Muffin pans, ramekins, and baking cups can be substituted for tartlet pans. You can either line these molds with dough on the inside in the usual way, or turn them upside down and line the outside. If you choose the latter, use *Flaky Cream Cheese Pastry Dough, 18;* other doughs have a tendency to melt and split during baking.

ABOUT
CRUSTS

*S*ome people are intimidated by the prospect of making a home-made pie crust, so instead, they rush to the supermarket and purchase ready-made dough. While these products are certainly convenient in a pinch, they pale in comparison to a pie crust you made yourself.

If you're looking for simplicity, try Pat-in-the-Pan Butter Crust, 26, *and* Crumb Crust, 30. *The more experienced baker will be delighted with recipes for* Deluxe Butter Flaky Pastry Dough, 17, *and* Meringue Pie Crust, 31. *While most dough is quick and easy to make by hand, the food processor makes short work of some recipes, 16.*

The step-by-step illustrations in this chapter take the guesswork out of making tarts and pies. You will learn how to mix, roll, shape, and bake crusts from the simplest to the most elegant.

Deluxe Butter Flaky Pastry Dough (Pâte Brisée), 17

Flaky Pastry (Pâte Brisée)

Well-made flaky pastry is a paradox—firm and crisp on the one hand but tender, light, and flaky on the other. It derives its strength from gluten, a tough, weblike structure that forms when flour is moistened with water and then handled during the mixing and rolling of the dough. For tenderness, pie pastry depends on fat, which, if properly mixed, prevents too much gluten from developing and separates the dough into paper-thin sheets, helping to create the flaky effect. No one recipe can precisely convey a sense of the way the dough should look and feel at all stages nor confer the fabled "touch." This comes (and it does come) only with practice. Still, flaky pastry is much less difficult to make than a novice baker often imagines. What follows is a step-by-step overview of the entire process.

Making Flaky Pastry Dough

There are two steps in the making of flaky pastry dough. In the first step, the goal is to cut the fat into the dry ingredients either by chopping vigorously with a pastry blender (below) or by cutting in opposite directions with 2 knives, one held in each hand. This leaves the fat in firm, separate pieces, some fine and crumblike and the rest the size of peas. The finer particles of fat coat the grains of flour, partially blocking the penetration of water and hindering the formation of gluten. The larger chunks of fat melt during baking, leaving gaps in the dough that fill up with steam and expand, and separating the pastry into myriad flaky ledges. Inexperienced pie makers tend to overwork the flour and fat mixture into a soft, greasy paste, resulting in pastry that is mealy and dense, like shortbread, rather than crisp and flaky. The age-old advice remains the best: Have the butter or lard cold (solid vegetable shortening, which resists melting, may be at room temperature) and work quickly and purposefully.

In the second step, the binding of the dough with water, the trick is to add enough water to make the dough cohere but not so much as to cause gluten to form, which will produce pastry that is either hard or chewy and breadlike. The amount of water required varies depending on the moisture content of the flour, the type of fat used, the degree of blending of fat and flour, and the ambient temperature and humidity. As a general rule, the flour and fat mixture should be moistened only to the point where it forms small balls that hold together when pressed together with your fingers. If the mixture gathers into a mass on its own, without pressure, it is too wet. Beginners should probably err on the side of overmoistening, as a very dry dough will split or crumble when rolled.

Flaky Pastry Dough

*Two 9-inch pie crusts, or two 9½-
or 10-inch tart crusts, or one 9-inch
covered pie crust*

*This dough makes a light, flaky crust
that crumbles delicately at the touch
of a fork. Before beginning, please read
Flaky Pastry, opposite, and Making
Flaky Pastry Dough, opposite. If you
want to make the dough in a food
processor, see page 16. If you need only
a single pie or tart crust, decrease all
ingredients by half or freeze half the
dough for future use.*

Using a rubber spatula, thoroughly
mix in a large bowl:

2½ cups all-purpose flour

**1 teaspoon white sugar or 1 table-
    spoon powdered sugar**

1 teaspoon salt

Add:

**1 cup solid vegetable shortening,
    or ½ cup shortening and 8 table-
    spoons (1 stick) cold unsalted
    butter**

Break the shortening into large
chunks; if using butter, cut it into
small pieces, then add it to the flour
mixture. Using a pastry blender or
2 knives, cut the fat into the dry
ingredients. As you work, periodically stir dry flour up from the
bottom of the bowl and scrape
clinging fat off the pastry blender
or knives. When you are through,
some of the fat should remain in
pea-sized pieces; the rest should be
reduced to the consistency of coarse
crumbs or cornmeal. The mixture
should seem dry and powdery and
not pasty or greasy. Drizzle over the
flour and fat mixture:

⅓ cup plus 1 tablespoon ice water

Using the rubber spatula, cut with
the blade side until the mixture looks
evenly moistened and begins to form

small balls. Press down on the dough
with the flat side of the spatula. If
the balls of dough stick together,
you have added enough water; if
they do not, drizzle over the top:

1 to 2 tablespoons ice water

Cut in the water, again using the
blade of the spatula, then press with
your hands until the dough coheres.
The dough should look rough, not
smooth. Divide the dough in half,
press each half into a thick, flat
disk, and wrap tightly in plastic.
Refrigerate for at least 30 minutes,

and preferably for several hours, or
for up to 2 days before rolling. The
dough can also be wrapped airtight
and frozen for up to 6 months; thaw
completely before rolling.

LARD FLAKY PASTRY DOUGH

*This very tender crust is best
reserved for covered fruit pies.
Prepare Flaky Pastry Dough, above,
substituting 1 cup of cold or frozen
lard, cut into pieces, for the fat.*

Fats Used in Flaky Pastry Dough

Solid vegetable shortening is easy to work with, because it resists melting and disperses easily in dry ingredients. It also has a tenderizing effect on flour and thus assures a tender crust. Shortening, however, has little flavor; use it in combination with unsalted butter if you want more flavor in the crust. For a very buttery crust, make *Deluxe Butter Flaky Pastry*

Dough, 17, which is almost entirely butter. Leaf lard, rendered from the fat of the pig that surrounds the kidneys, produces a wonderfully flaky crust and is traditional for covered fruit pies but is difficult to find. Supermarket lard, which is processed from various parts of the animal, has a more pronounced flavor than leaf lard.

To measure bulk fats, like shortening, butter, or leaf lard, use the displacement method. If you put these fats in dry measuring cups, pockets of air can form and throw off the measurement. Instead, if you want ½ cup shortening, fill a 1-cup liquid measure half full with water, then add the fat until the water reaches the 1-cup mark. Pour off the water.

HOW TO MAKE FLAKY PASTRY DOUGH USING A FOOD PROCESSOR

These instructions pertain to Flaky Pastry Dough, 15, Deluxe Butter Flaky Pastry Dough, 17, and their variations, as well as to Flaky Cream Cheese Pastry Dough, 18. Have all fats and cream cheese cold, preferably frozen.

1 Combine the dry ingredients in the food processor and process for 10 seconds. Cut the fat (and cream cheese) into ½-inch chunks and, with the machine off, scatter over the top.

2 Pulse in 1- to 2-second bursts until most of the fat is the size of peas.

3 With the machine turned off, drizzle the liquid evenly over the top. Pulse until no dry patches remain and the dough begins to clump into small balls.

4 Try to press the dough together with your fingers; if it will not cohere, sprinkle on a bit more liquid, pulse, and try again. Do not allow the dough to gather into a single mass during processing. Wrap and refrigerate as directed.

Deluxe Butter Flaky Pastry Dough (Pâte Brisée)

Two 9-inch pie crusts, or two 9½- or 10-inch tart crusts, or one 9-inch covered pie crust

This dough is richer in fat than ordinary flaky pastry and is thus softer and more difficult to handle, but it yields a marvelously tender, flaky crust with a superb butter flavor. While it is possible to make this dough with butter only, a small amount of shortening makes it flakier without interfering with the buttery taste. Since this dough tends to puff out of shape during baking, you should not use it to make a crust with a tightly fluted or braided edge. Before beginning, please read Flaky Pastry, 14, *and* Making Flaky Pastry Dough, 14. *If you want to make this in a food processor, see opposite. If you need only a single pie or tart crust, decrease all ingredients by half or freeze half the dough for future use.*

Using a rubber spatula, thoroughly mix in a large bowl:

2½ cups all-purpose flour

1 teaspoon white sugar or 1 tablespoon powdered sugar

1 teaspoon salt

Working quickly to prevent softening, cut into ¼-inch pieces:

½ pound (2 sticks) cold unsalted butter

Add the butter to the dry ingredients. Using a pastry blender or 2 knives, chop the butter into pea-sized pieces. Add:

¼ cup solid vegetable shortening

With a few quick swipes of the pastry blender, cut the shortening into large chunks and distribute throughout the bowl. Continue to chop until the mixture resembles coarse crumbs with some pea-sized pieces. Do not let the mixture soften and begin to clump; it must remain dry and powdery. Drizzle over the flour and fat mixture:

⅓ cup plus 1 tablespoon ice water

Cut with the blade side of the rubber spatula until the mixture looks evenly moistened and begins to form small balls. Press down on the dough with the flat side of the spatula. If the balls of dough stick together, you have added enough water; if they do not, drizzle over the top:

1 to 2 tablespoons ice water

Cut in the water, then press with your hands until the dough coheres. The dough should look rough, not smooth. Divide the dough in half, press each half into a thick, flat disk, and wrap tightly in plastic. Refrigerate for at least 30 minutes, preferably for several hours, or for up to 2 days before rolling. The dough can also be wrapped airtight and frozen for up to 6 months; thaw completely before rolling.

BUTTER

Use all store-bought butter within 1 week of the date stamped on the carton. Because butter readily absorbs odors, store it well wrapped in the refrigerator and away from other foods. Unopened unsalted butter lasts about 8 weeks, salted up to 12. Use all opened butter within 3 weeks. You also can freeze butter for up to 6 months.

CORNMEAL FLAKY PASTRY DOUGH

Cornmeal adds crunch and lightness to crusts. Use for fresh fruit tarts made with berries, peaches, or nectarines.
Prepare *Deluxe Butter Flaky Pastry Dough, left,* substituting ¾ cup yellow cornmeal for ¾ cup of the all-purpose flour and increasing the powdered sugar to ⅓ cup.

NUT FLAKY PASTRY DOUGH

Prepare *Deluxe Butter Flaky Pastry Dough, left,* adding ½ cup finely chopped or coarsely ground walnuts or pecans to the dry ingredients and increasing the powdered sugar to ⅓ cup. You can also add 1 teaspoon grated lemon zest with the nuts.

SWEET FLAKY PASTRY DOUGH

This pastry is delicious but burns easily. Use it only for pies and tarts that require little or no baking after being filled.
Prepare *Deluxe Butter Flaky Pastry Dough, left,* increasing the powdered sugar to ¾ cup.

WHOLE-WHEAT FLAKY PASTRY DOUGH

Prepare *Deluxe Butter Flaky Pastry Dough, left,* substituting 1 cup whole-wheat pastry flour for 1 cup of the all-purpose flour and increasing the powdered sugar to ⅓ cup. For extra tenderness, beat in 1 large egg yolk with the first addition of ice water.

Flaky Cream Cheese Pastry Dough

One 9- or 10-inch pie crust or 9½- or 10-inch tart crust

Cream cheese pastry is rich and tangy, and it seems to turn out tender and flaky no matter what. To make this in a food processor, see page 16. This recipe can be doubled and used to make a covered or lattice-top pie. Use this dough when making tartlet crusts, since it will hold its shape better during baking than other flaky pastry doughs.

Whisk together in a large bowl:

**1 cup plus 2 tablespoons
   all-purpose flour**

**1 tablespoon white sugar or 2
   tablespoons powdered sugar**

¼ teaspoon salt

Cut into ¼-inch pieces and add:

**6 tablespoons (¾ stick) cold
   unsalted butter**

3 ounces cold cream cheese

Using a pastry blender or 2 knives, cut the butter and cream cheese into

the dry ingredients until the mixture resembles coarse crumbs with some pea-sized pieces. Drizzle over the top:

2 to 3 tablespoons cold heavy cream

Cut with the blade side of a rubber spatula or stir with a fork until the dough begins to gather into moist clumps. Press the dough into a thick, flat disk, wrap tightly in plastic, and refrigerate for at least 1 hour or up to 2 days.

SWEETENING AND FLAVORING FLAKY PASTRY DOUGHS

Our basic recipes for *Flaky Pastry Dough*, 15, and *Deluxe Butter Flaky Pastry Dough*, 17, call for just a hint of sugar. However, both doughs can be sweetened more if you prefer. Except when used in tiny amounts, ordinary granulated sugar makes flaky pastry doughs sticky and hard to handle, so use powdered sugar instead. One-quarter to ⅓ cup powdered sugar to 2½ cups of flour will impart a light background sweetness; ¾ cup will make the crust noticeably sweet.

Crusts made with more than ¾ cup powdered sugar may burn and turn out crunchy rather than flaky.

You may flavor any flaky pastry dough by whisking one or more of the following into the flour and other dry ingredients. With all these additions, you should sweeten the dough with at least ¼ cup powdered sugar. These amounts are for a full recipe of Flaky Pastry Dough or Deluxe Butter Flaky Pastry Dough; use only half as much if

you are halving the recipe or if you are making Flaky Cream Cheese Pastry Dough, above.

Nuts: ⅓ to ½ cup coarsely ground or finely chopped

Sesame or poppy seeds: 2 tablespoons

Anise, caraway, or coriander seeds: 1 tablespoon finely crushed

Orange or lemon zest: 1 to 2 teaspoons grated

Cinnamon, ginger, cardamom, or nutmeg: ¼ teaspoon ground

HOW TO ROLL OUT PASTRY DOUGH

The secret to rolling dough is to lean into the pin rather than down on it: The goal is to enlarge the dough, not to press and crush it. You can roll dough on a wood or plastic pastry board or on a marble slab (which retains cold and thus helps keep the dough from softening) or directly on a clean smooth countertop. Do not roll dough next to the oven or in a hot corner of the kitchen, or the fat will melt. If the dough has been chilled for longer than 30 minutes, let it stand until it feels firm yet pliable. If too cold, the dough will crack around the edges when rolled. If the dough becomes too soft during rolling, slide a rimless cookie sheet beneath it and refrigerate until it firms up.

1 Flour the work surface—lightly if you are an experienced pastry maker but a bit more generously if you are starting out. Excessive flouring toughens dough, but sticking is a disaster. Place the dough in the center of the floured surface and flour the dough as well.

2 Exerting even pressure on the pin, roll the dough from the center out in all directions, stopping just short of the edge. In order to keep the dough in a circular shape, each stroke should be made in the opposite direction from the one that preceded it. You can do this by rotating the dough itself rather than by moving the pin. If the dough assumes an irregular shape, cut off the protruding piece, moisten the edge with cold water and press it over the short spot. Check the dough for sticking periodically; strew a little flour on the work surface as necessary.

3 Seal cracks and splits by pressing the dough together. If the split reopens, your dough is probably too dry. Dab the edges of the split with cold water, overlap the edges slightly, and press firmly with your fingertips, sprinkling a little flour over the repaired area if it feels moist and sticky.

4 Roll the dough 3 to 4 inches wider than your pan. This will allow plenty of dough for constructing a rim. Place the pan (right side up for a tart pan, inverted for a pie pan) in the center of the dough to calculate the width by eye. (For beginners and those who find sticking a problem, see step 3 of *How to Pat Dough into the Pan, 27,* for instructions on rolling dough between 2 pieces of waxed paper.

HOW TO FIT THE DOUGH INTO THE PAN

1 Transfer the dough to the pan by rolling it loosely around the pin. Center the pin over the pan, and then unroll the dough.

2 Alternatively, you can fold the dough in halves or quarters, place it in the pan, and unfold it to cover. It is important to press the dough over the bottom and into the corners before you mold it against the pan sides. Otherwise, you will end up with stretched corners that may tear when the shell is weighted for prebaking or is filled.

3 Patch any holes or cracks with dough scraps, first lightly moistening the scraps with cold water.

4 When you are satisfied that the pan is completely covered, trim the edges of the dough with scissors, leaving an overhang of ¾ inch all around the sides of the pan. Wrap and refrigerate all scraps. These will come in handy if the shell shrinks or splits when baked.

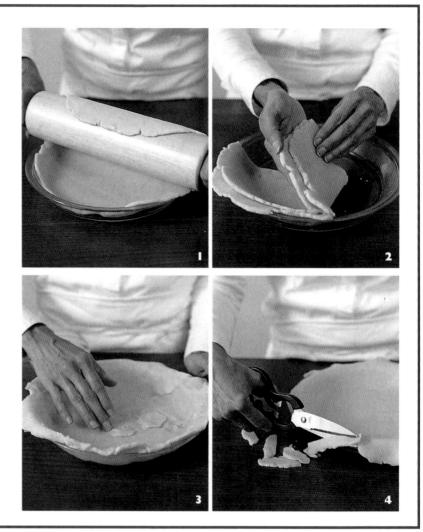

Resting, Storing, and Freezing Unbaked Crusts

In order to relax the dough and minimize shrinkage, pie and tart crusts must be chilled for at least 30 minutes before baking. A rest of 3 to 24 hours is preferable if you have designed an elaborate crust rim. To keep the pastry from drying out, wrap crusts that are refrigerated for more than 3 hours in plastic or cover with the foil liner to be used in weighting the shell, 22. A crust may also be frozen for up to 6 months. Either freeze it in the pan, wrapped airtight in foil and then sealed in a plastic bag, or freeze it solid, then pry it out of the pan and wrap. Frozen crusts need not be thawed before baking. They will require a few minutes longer in the oven.

HOW TO MAKE A PIE OR TART CRUST

The following directions apply to any flaky pastry dough.

1 *To Make a Pie Crust:* Tuck the over-hanging ¾ inch of pastry dough underneath itself to make a doubled rim, then rest the rim on the flared edge of the pie pan.

2 To crimp the rim, press it all around with the tines of a fork or the blunt side of a knife.

3 For a fluted rim, press your thumb and index finger, held about 1 inch apart, against the outside of the rim, then poke a dent through the space from the inside of the pie crust with the index finger of your other hand. Continue evenly all around the rim of the pan.

4 For a coiled or braided design on the rim, roll dough trimmings into long thin ropes, then twist or braid the ropes to your choosing.

Flatten the rim of the pie crust against the edge of the pan, brush the rim with cold water, and press the fancy rope into place.

5 *To Make a Tart Crust:* Lightly brush the sides of the tart crust with cold water. Fold the dough overhanging the pan down over the sides and press firmly, doubling the thickness of the upper part of the crust wall.

6 Squeeze any noticeably thicker parts of the sides towards the top of the pan with your fingers, then trim the protruding spots flush with the rest of the top using kitchen scissors.

Prebaking and Weighting Crusts

In previous editions of JOY, we called for only *partial* prebaking of flaky pastry crusts that would be returned to the oven and baked again with the filling, as in pumpkin or pecan pie. Our theory was that the second baking would finish what the first had begun, but time and time again, our theory was refuted by a soggy, undercooked crust. We now believe that all prebaked pastry crusts must be fully baked before filling. Defying logic, the baked shells do not burn when baked a second time with their filling, though the edge does sometimes darken—a small price to pay for a deliciously crisp and flaky crust.

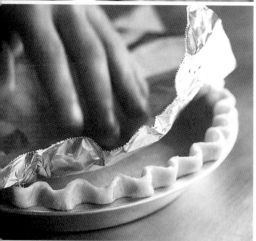

When pastry crusts are baked unfilled—"blind baked"—they tend to puff up and slip down the sides of the pan unless weighted with raw beans or rice or metal pie weights (top photo) during the first 20 minutes of baking. Instead of using weights, you may keep the dough in place by nesting a pie pan of identical size in the crust. If you choose this method, you must be content with a simple crimped rim, for the second pan will flatten a fluted or braided rim.

Baked Flaky Pastry Crust

One 9-inch pie crust or 9½- or 10-inch tart crust

The pastry doughs listed here are all-purpose doughs and may be used interchangeably in any recipe calling for a baked flaky pastry crust. Before beginning, please read How to Roll Out Pastry Dough, 19, *and* Prebaking and Weighting Crusts, above.

Prepare:

½ recipe Flaky Pastry Dough, 15,
    ½ recipe Deluxe Butter Flaky Pastry Dough, 17, or 1 recipe Flaky Cream Cheese Pastry Dough, 18

Roll out the dough and fit it into a 9-inch pie pan or 9½- or 10-inch two-piece tart pan. Refrigerate the crust for at least 30 minutes. Position a rack in the lower third of the oven. Preheat the oven to 400°F. Smooth a sheet of heavy-duty aluminum foil, shiny side down, over the bottom and sides of the crust, flaring the excess foil, like an awning, over the crust edge to keep it from overbrowning. Fill the liner with raw beans or rice or metal pie weights, banking the weights against the sides of the crust if you do not have enough to fill the crust to the brim. Bake the crust for 20 minutes. Carefully lift out the foil with the weights inside. Prick the crust thoroughly with a fork, return it to the oven, and bake until the crust is golden brown all over, 5 to 10 minutes more. Check the crust periodically; if it puffs along the bottom, prick it with a fork, then press down gently with the back of a spoon. If you are filling the crust with an uncooked mixture that requires further baking, whisk together, then brush the inside with:

1 large egg yolk
Pinch of salt

Return to the oven until the egg glaze sets, 1 to 2 minutes. Fill the shell at once, while still hot, or let cool as specified in the recipe.

Baked Flaky Pastry Tartlet Crusts

About nine 3½-inch or six 4½-inch crusts

Tartlet pans come in an array of sizes, shapes, and designs. The following instructions assume that you will be using 3½- to 4½-inch pans with shallow, straight sides, which produce crusts of a size suitable for individual first-course or dessert tartlets. If you are using smaller, slope-sided pans to make dessert-tray tartlets or hors d'oeuvre cases, roll the dough thinner (¹/₁₆ inch, if you can manage it) and do not double the crust sides. Obviously, the baking times and yield will also vary.

While it is possible to make tartlet crusts with Flaky Pastry Dough, 15, *or even* Deluxe Butter Flaky Pastry Dough, 17, *these doughs tend to both* *puff and shrink down the sides of the pans during baking, diminishing the holding capacity of the crusts. These problems can be solved by prebaking the crusts with weights, as one does for large shells. We prefer cream cheese pastry dough for tartlet shells, since it holds its shape better during baking.*

Prepare:

Flaky Cream Cheese Pastry Dough, 18

On a lightly floured work surface, roll the dough about ⅛ inch thick, then cut into rounds wide enough to cover the bottom and sides of your tartlet pans, with 1 to 1½ inches extra dough to spare. Press the dough rounds into the pans, then fold the overhanging dough back on itself over the crust sides, doubling their thickness. Press the doubled dough firmly to seal, then thoroughly prick the sides and bottoms with a fork. Arrange the crusts on a baking sheet and refrigerate for at least 30 minutes.

Position a rack in the center of the oven. Preheat the oven to 400°F. Bake the crusts for 5 to 7 minutes, then prick the bottoms of any that have puffed. Continue to bake until the crusts are golden brown and firm to the touch, 12 to 15 minutes more. Cool completely and unmold before filling.

Moisture-proofing the Crust

Crusts that are to hold uncooked fillings and then be baked should be glazed with egg yolk to prevent sogginess: Whisk together 1 large egg yolk and a pinch of salt. Use a pastry brush to lightly coat the bottom and sides of the crust with the glaze. Baked crusts that will be filled with cooked mixtures can be glazed with yolk or, if the filling will be poured in cold, glazed with one of the following:

Fruit glaze: Melt jelly, jam, or preserves in a small saucepan over low heat, then strain out any solids. Brush the warm glaze over the bottom and the sides of the shell. If you are making a fresh fruit tart, you can brush the fruits on top of the tart with the same glaze that you applied to the shell.

Butter: Unsalted butter makes an effective and virtually unnoticeable protective coat. Soften about

2 teaspoons of unsalted butter to the consistency of mayonnaise, then brush or spread it very thinly over the bottom and sides of the baked shell.

Chocolate: Melt semisweet, bittersweet, milk, or white chocolate, and spread it thinly over the inside of the crust with a knife or the back of a spoon. Refrigerate the crust until the chocolate hardens. Moisture-proof shells with chocolate only when its flavor is compatible with the pie or tart filling.

Chocolate Ganache Glaze, below: This is as effective as chocolate in moisture-proofing a shell and, because it is soft, may be applied in a much thicker layer. Banana cream pie, peanut butter pie, and fresh raspberry tarts are particularly good with ganache-glazed shells.

Chocolate Ganache Glaze
About 1½ cups

Ganache is a French term that refers to any combination of chocolate and cream. It is smooth on the palate and rich in flavor.

Bring to a boil in a small saucepan:

¾ cup heavy cream

Remove from the heat and add:

8 ounces semisweet or bittersweet chocolate, finely chopped

Stir until most of the chocolate is melted. Cover and let stand for 10 minutes. Stir or whisk very gently until completely smooth. Stir in:

1 tablespoon liqueur, or more to taste (optional)

For a pourable glaze, let stand at room temperature, stirring occasionally, until the mixture cools to 85° to 95°F. For frosting, let stand until spreadable. If the frosting becomes too stiff, set the pan in a larger pan of hot water and stir until softened; or remelt and cool to 85° to 95°F for use as a glaze. This keeps for up to 3 days at room temperature, 1 week refrigerated, or 3 months frozen. Soften or melt before using.

HOW TO PATCH A BLIND-BAKED CRUST

Pastry crusts sometimes develop a split along the bottom (usually during the weighted phase of baking) or shrink down the sides of the pan (usually after the weights have been removed). If the crust is to hold a thick, fully cooked mixture—as in cream, chiffon, or lemon meringue pie—small imperfections can be ignored. But if you are filling the crust with an uncooked liquid mixture—as in custard, pecan, chess, or pumpkin pie—*all cracks need to be patched, or the filling will leak through.*

1 Using your fingertips, press the reserved dough scraps into the required shape, lightly moisten one side with water, and press the moistened side over the problem area of the baked crust.

2 If you have no scraps, make a thick paste with flour and water and smear it with your fingers or the back of a small spoon over the tear. The crust needs to be returned to the oven only long enough to harden and dry the patch, not to brown it and bake it through.

3 If glazing the crust with egg yolk before filling, be sure that the edges of the patch are completely sealed with yolk.

Pat-in-the-Pan Crusts

The success of flaky pastry depends upon the expert management of gluten. Pat-in-the-pan doughs are made in such a way that virtually no gluten develops. The fat is softened and thoroughly blended into the flour, not cut in as for flaky pastry dough. As a result, the flour ends up moisture-proofed by the fat and can-not absorb the liquid needed to produce gluten. All pat-in-the-pan crusts are crumbly, rather than flaky.

Pat-in-the-pan crusts are usually baked before they are filled. Therefore they cannot be used to make covered fruit pies, though short-bread doughs can be used to make the flat, free-form dessert tarts known as galettes (or, in Italian, *crostatas*). Note also that these crusts must be glazed with egg yolk or another glaze (see *Moisture-proofing the Crust*, 24) when they are to be filled and further baked, as in pecan or pumpkin pies; otherwise, the crusts will soak up the filling and adhere to the pan.

Pat-in-the-Pan Butter Crust

One 9-inch pie or 9½- or 10-inch tart crust

Those who are daunted by flaky pastry will find this simple alternative more than satisfactory.

This dough will also make about eight 3½-inch tartlet crusts. Press the dough over the bottom and up the sides of the tartlet molds and bake until firm and golden, about 15 minutes, pricking the dough several times during baking with a fork.

Position a rack in the center of the oven. Preheat the oven to 400°F. Whisk together in a bowl or process for 10 seconds in a food processor:

1½ cups all-purpose flour
½ teaspoon salt

Add:

8 tablespoons (1 stick) unsalted butter, softened, cut into 8 pieces

Mash with the back of a fork or process in a food processor until the mixture resembles coarse crumbs. Drizzle over the top:

2 to 3 tablespoons heavy cream

Stir or process until the crumbs look damp and hold together when pinched. Transfer the mixture to a 9-inch pie pan or 9½- or 10-inch two-piece tart pan (opposite). Pat evenly over the bottom and sides with your fingertips. If making a pie, form a crust edge and crimp or flute. Prick the bottom and sides with a fork. Bake until the crust is golden brown, 18 to 22 minutes, pricking the bottom once or twice if it bubbles. If you are filling the crust with an uncooked mixture that requires further baking, whisk together:

1 large egg yolk
Pinch of salt

Brush the inside of the crust with the egg yolk glaze. Return to the oven and bake until the egg glaze sets, 1 to 2 minutes.

HOW TO PAT DOUGH INTO THE PAN

Although patting out a crust is a simple procedure, it must be done carefully if the crust is to be of an even thickness. Start by patting the dough into an even 4-inch disk. If it is soft and sticky, refrigerate it until it becomes manageable; if it is cold and hard, let it stand at room temperature until malleable, like modeling clay. If you are comfortable and proficient with the pin, you may find it easier to produce a crust of an even thickness by rolling the dough rather than patting it. Since these doughs tend to be sticky, soft, and crumbly, they must be rolled between sheets of wax paper.

1 Set the dough in the center of your pie or tart pan. Always working from the center out, press down on the dough in all directions until it covers the entire bottom of the pan in an even layer.

To form the sides of the crust, again press the dough from the center of the pan in all directions until an even ring of dough builds up against the pan sides. Evenly flatten the dough ring against the pan sides to form the crust sides.

In forming a pie crust, you can push the top of the sides slightly beyond the rim of the pan and crimp or flute the crust edge.

2 For a tart crust, press down on the top of the sides with the thumb of one hand while pressing against the inside edge with the forefinger of your other hand. You will thus make the top of the sides flat and of the same thickness as the base, which not only strengthens the sides but also gives the crust an attractive look.

3 To roll out the dough, lightly flour both sides of the dough and set it between two 12-inch squares of wax paper. Working from the center out, roll the dough into a 12-inch circle. If the paper wrinkles as you roll, peel it off and smooth it back into place.

Remove the top sheet of wax paper. Holding the bottom sheet by the corners, pick up the dough and flip it, paper side up, into the pan, then carefully peel off the paper.

4 The dough may not end up centered in the pan, and it may tear and crumble, but none of this matters. Simply press the dough into the pan's contours and then repair any holes by pushing the dough together with your fingers. Finish the edge of the crust as directed above.

Shortbread Crust

One 9-inch pie or 9½- or 10-inch tart crust

This rich, sweet dough resembles a shortbread cookie. Use it for a cream pie, a lemon tart, a fresh fruit tart with pastry cream, or any other pie or tart with a creamy or buttery filling, or to make approximately eight 3½-inch tartlet crusts. For tartlets, press the dough into your molds and bake until firm and golden, about 15 minutes, pricking with a fork several times during baking. If you make this in a food processor using cold butter, it will be firm enough to form into a crust at once; if made by hand with softened butter, the dough will require brief chilling before forming.

Position a rack in the center of the oven. Preheat the oven to 400°F. Grease or butter the bottom, but not the sides, of a 9-inch pie pan or 9½- or 10-inch two-piece tart pan. Dust the pan with flour, tilt to coat the bottom, then tap out the excess. (If using a tart pan, pop out the bottom, wedge it between your palms, and tap.)

Whisk together in a bowl or process for 10 seconds in a food processor:

1¼ cups all-purpose flour
⅓ cup sugar
1 teaspoon grated lemon zest (optional)
¼ teaspoon salt

Add:

8 tablespoons (1 stick) unsalted butter, softened if working by hand, cut into 8 pieces

Mash with the back of a fork or process until the mixture resembles coarse crumbs. Add:

1 large egg yolk

Mix with a spatula or process just until the dough comes together in a ball. If the dough is too soft and sticky to work with, refrigerate for at least 30 minutes or up to 2 days. Pat the dough evenly over the bottom and sides of the prepared pan, or roll it between sheets of wax paper and flip it into the pan (see *How to Pat Dough into the Pan, 27*). Do not attempt to crimp or flute the edge. Thoroughly prick the bottom and sides with a fork. Bake until deep golden brown, 18 to 22 minutes. If you are filling the crust with an uncooked mixture that requires further baking, whisk together, then brush the inside with:

1 large egg yolk
Pinch of salt

Return to the oven until the egg glaze sets, 1 to 2 minutes.

Vegetable Oil Crust

One 9-inch pie or 9½- or 10-inch tart crust

This firm, sandy-textured crust is easier to roll than to pat. The flavor of the oil tends to become pronounced with prolonged baking, so save this crust for pies that don't need to be baked after filling, such as cream pies, Key lime pie, or lemon meringue pie.

Position a rack in the lower third of the oven. Preheat the oven to 425°F. Whisk together thoroughly:

1⅓ cups all-purpose flour
½ teaspoon salt

Mix in a cup until creamy:

⅓ cup plus 1 tablespoon vegetable oil
¼ cup cold milk

Pour the oil mixture over the dry ingredients and stir with a fork until blended. Pat the dough evenly over the bottom and sides of a 9-inch pie pan or 9½- or 10-inch two-piece tart pan, or roll it between sheets of wax paper and flip it into the pan (see *How to Pat Dough into the Pan*, 27). If making a pie, crimp or flute the edge. Thoroughly prick the sides and bottom with a fork. Bake until the crust is golden brown, 12 to 18 minutes. If you are filling the crust with an uncooked mixture that requires further baking, whisk together, then brush the inside with:

1 large egg yolk
Pinch of salt

Return to the oven until the egg glaze sets, 1 to 2 minutes.

Gluten-Free Crust

Two 9-inch pie crusts

Many people love this wheat-free crust because it is easy to make, freezes well, and tastes like French tart dough. You may sprinkle the scraps with cinnamon and sugar and bake them into cookies, if you wish. Xanthan gum can be found in health-food stores and online. Remember to have the cream cheese and eggs at room temperature before you start.

Pulse 4 or 5 times in a food processor to combine:

1 cup white rice flour
¾ cup potato starch
½ cup tapioca flour
1 tablespoon sugar
1 teaspoon salt
¼ teaspoon xanthan gum

Add and process until well blended:

4 ounces cream cheese, softened, cut into cubes
½ cup vegetable shortening

Add and process until a smooth dough forms:

1 large egg, at room temperature
2 large egg yolks, at room temperature
1 teaspoon gluten-free vanilla

3 tablespoons very cold tap water

You may shape and bake the pie crusts immediately or freeze the dough.

To bake immediately, lightly grease two 9-inch pans. With wet hands, place half the dough in each pan. Evenly pat the dough across the bottom and up the sides, and form a rim at the top. Decorate the rim by pressing it with the tines of a fork. Prick the shell all over with a fork. Freeze while preheating the oven to 425°F. Bake until the edges are golden brown, about 15 minutes.

To freeze and bake at a later date, divide the dough in half and place each half on a large sheet of plastic wrap. Pat each into a ½-inch-thick-disk. Cover tightly with the plastic wrap, place in freezer bags, and freeze for up to 3 months. When you are ready to use it, thaw the dough for about 1½ hours at room temperature. Sprinkle potato starch lightly over a large sheet of parchment paper and a rolling pin. Place one disk of dough on the parchment and roll from the center out to a 10-inch round. Invert a 9-inch pie pan over the dough and invert the parchment with the dough into the pan. Pat the dough evenly in the pan, removing the paper. Shape a rim and prick all over with a fork. Bake as directed above.

Crumb and Nut Crusts

The sweet crunchiness of these easy-to-make crusts provides a delicious contrast to creamy fillings. Graham crackers are the usual base, but chocolate and vanilla wafers, gingersnaps, and zwieback also make wonderful crumb crusts. If you are starting with crackers or cookies, grind them in a food processor or put them in a sturdy plastic bag and pulverize them with a rolling pin. The crumbs must be quite fine, or the crust is likely to crumble when cut. You can freeze these crusts for 20 minutes before filling and not bake them, but they are indisputably crunchier and more flavorful when baked. Measure the butter and sugar carefully. If there is too little of either, the crumbs will not cohere when patted into the pan. If there is too much, the crust may slip down the sides of the pan during baking and turn out hard and candylike. (Should the crust slip or bubble during baking, it can usually be smoothed into place with the back of a spoon.) To prevent sticking, lightly grease or oil the pan before patting the crust into the pan. If the crust sticks nonetheless, set the bottom of the pan in a bowl of warm water for 1 minute.

Crumb Crust

One 10-inch pie crust

The proportions here are ample for a 10-inch pie pan or a 10- to 12-inch springform pan, and very generous for a 9-inch pie pan or an 8- to 9-inch springform pan. For the smaller size pans, you can reduce quantities to 1¼ cups crumbs, 5 tablespoons butter, and 3 tablespoons sugar.

If you wish to bake the crust, preheat the oven to 350°F. Lightly grease or oil a pie pan or springform pan.

Mix together with a fork or pulse in a food processor until all the ingredients are moistened:

1½ cups fine crumbs made from graham crackers, chocolate or vanilla wafers, or gingersnaps
6 tablespoons (¾ stick) melted butter, warm or cool
¼ cup sugar
¼ teaspoon ground cinnamon (optional)

Spread the mixture evenly in the pan. Using your fingertips or the flat bottom of a drinking glass, firmly press the mixture over the bottom and ½ inch up the sides of a pie pan or over the bottom of a springform pan. Freeze for 20 minutes or bake until the crust is lightly browned and firm to the touch, 10 to 15 minutes. Let cool thoroughly if filling with a cooked mixture, but use hot if filling with a mixture that requires baking.

Nut Crust

One 10-inch pie crust

To make this crust in a food processor, combine nut halves or pieces with the butter, sugar, and salt and pulse until the nuts are finely chopped.

Preheat the oven to 375°F. Grease a 9- or 10-inch pie pan or an 8- to 10-inch springform pan.

Chop to the consistency of coarse crumbs, either by hand or in a food processor:

2 cups walnuts or pecans

Add and mix with a fork until uniformly moistened:

4 tablespoons (½ stick) unsalted butter, softened
3 tablespoons sugar
¼ teaspoon salt

Using your fingertips or the flat bottom of a drinking glass, press the mixture evenly over the bottom and sides of a pie pan or over the bottom and ½ inch up the sides of a springform pan. Bake until the crust is richly browned, 10 to 15 minutes. Check the crust periodically during baking; if the crust has slipped down the sides of the pan, smooth it into place with the back of a spoon and continue baking. Let cool completely on a wire rack before filling.

Meringue Pie Crust

One 10-inch pie crust

Pure white, sweet, crisp, and fat free, meringue is an excellent crust for ice cream and frozen yogurt pies or for tarts made with fresh fruit and whipped cream. Meringue shells can be made in small pans of any size or formed on a baking sheet using a spoon or a pastry bag. Note the long baking—and long storing—time.

Position a rack in the lower third of the oven. Preheat the oven to 225°F. Very generously grease, with solid vegetable shortening, both the inside and the rim of a 10-inch pie pan, preferably glass. Dust the pan with flour, tilt in all directions to coat, then tap out the excess.

Prepare:

Soft Meringue Topping, right

Spread the meringue over the bottom and sides of the prepared pie pan with the back of a spoon. Bake until the interior of the meringue seems just slightly sticky when probed with the point of a paring knife, 1½ to 2 hours. Turn off the oven and let the crust cool completely inside the oven. Wrap the crust airtight and store at room temperature until needed. It will keep indefinitely. If it becomes soft during storage, bake unwrapped in a 200°F oven for 1 hour to recrisp.

Soft Meringue Topping

Covers one 9-inch pie or makes one 10-inch crust

This meringue is excellent for topping pies as well as making meringue crusts. Because it is stabilized by starch, when this meringue is used as a topping, it does not weep, leak, or deflate even when refrigerated for several days.

In a small saucepan thoroughly mix:

1 tablespoon cornstarch
1 tablespoon sugar

Gradually stir in, making a smooth, runny paste:

⅓ cup water

Bring to a boil over medium heat, stirring briskly all the while, then boil for 15 seconds until a thick, translucent paste is formed. Remove from the heat and cover with a lid or saucer. In a clean, grease-free glass or metal bowl, beat on medium speed until foamy:

4 large egg whites (½ cup), at room temperature

Add and beat until soft but definite peaks form:

½ teaspoon vanilla
¼ teaspoon cream of tartar

Very gradually beat in:

½ cup sugar, preferably superfine

Beat on high speed until the peaks are very stiff and glossy but not dry. Reduce the speed to low and beat in the cornstarch paste 1 tablespoon at a time. When all the paste is incorporated, increase the speed to medium and beat for 10 seconds. Bake as directed in your recipe.

ABOUT **COVERED** FRUIT PIES

A hundred years ago, fruit pies were eaten for breakfast as well as supper. During those times, American housewives often baked a dozen or more fruit pies every week. Today many home bakers have never made a covered fruit pie, but this chapter will teach you the basics and beyond.

Fruit pies are often less than picture perfect. They might bubble over during baking, brown unevenly, stick to the pan, or yield somewhat runny slices. No matter what you do you might also end up with a pie whose undercrust turns out slightly soft on the side facing the fruit. But don't be discouraged. These are normal occurrences in the baking of fruit pies, and certainly do not affect the unforgettable taste of an old-fashioned covered fruit pie.

Blueberry Pie, 40

Fillings for Fruit Pies

A covered fruit pie is simply fruit baked between two crusts, the upper one of which is a single pastry sheet or multiple strips of pastry arranged in a lattice. Other than the fruit, which may be canned, frozen, dried, or precooked as well as fresh and raw, the filling usually contains sugar and a thickener such as flour, cornstarch, or quick-cooking tapioca.

Older recipes, our own included, generally call for 4 cups of sliced fresh fruit or berries for a 9-inch fruit pie, which is the approximate amount that a standard 9-inch pie pan will hold when lined with pastry. However, since raw fruit shrinks when cooked, we now prefer to start with 5 cups of fruit, or even more in the case of apples, to ensure that the top crust will not sink and the filling will seem ample. The measuring cup should be leveled, not heaped. Although it is possible (and tempting) to mound 6 to 7 cups of fruit into a 9-inch crust, it is not wise to do so, for the pie is certain to gush juices as it bakes, and it may not hold together well when sliced.

Ideally, the amount of sugar and thickener added to the filling should be adjusted according to the sweetness, acidity, and juiciness of the fruit. Sugar is a simple issue, but deciding how much thickener to add is tricky. In general, we lean toward the lesser quantity of thickener suggested in the recipes when there is a choice given. However, if you are partial to pies that slice neatly and are willing to risk a slightly solid filling, add the greater amount of thickener called for.

While flour is still a popular choice for thickener among home cooks, cornstarch or quick-cooking tapioca produces clearer fillings and a smoother, more melting consistency. The exception is apple pie, which seems to benefit from the creaminess that flour imparts. Of course, you may thicken any fruit pie with flour. Use twice as much flour as cornstarch or tapioca.

Once mixed, fruit pie fillings should not stand longer than 15 minutes before being turned into the crust, or else they may become too juicy.

CORNSTARCH AND TAPIOCA

A pure starch with almost twice the thickening power of flour, cornstarch is an excellent and relatively unobtrusive thickening agent. Unlike flour, it adds no floury taste.

Tapioca is derived from the root of the tropical cassava plant, which in many parts of the world is boiled and eaten as a starch. Most supermarkets today carry quick-cooking tapioca, a precooked form that comes in tiny grains and is used to thicken fruit pie fillings.

If you are making a pie with a lattice top, it's best to use cornstarch rather than quick-cooking tapioca. The exposed tapioca grains sometimes do not cook and melt into the fruit, resulting in a watery, grainy filling bubbling over the lattice strips.

Crusts for Fruit Pies

Crusts for covered fruit pies must be made with a flaky pastry dough. *Flaky Pastry Dough*, 15, made either with shortening or with a combination of butter and shortening, and *Deluxe Butter Flaky Pastry Dough*, 17, are suitable for any fruit pie. *Lard Flaky Pastry Dough*, 15, is particularly good with apple pies but works as well with other fruit pies, so long as you appreciate the flavor of lard. *Flaky Cream Cheese Pastry Dough*, 18, is also a good all-purpose dough, though you may find it a bit too tangy with tart fruits such as sour cherries and rhubarb. If you like, use *Cornmeal Flaky Pastry Dough*, 17, for blueberry or blackberry pies or *Nut Flaky Pastry Dough*, 17, with stone fruits, such as peaches or cherries. Be aware, however, that these doughs tend to leak during baking. *Sweet Flaky Pastry Dough*, 17, is not good for covered fruit pies, as it is likely to char during the long baking.

In making the dough for a covered fruit pie, it is better to add slightly more liquid than is needed rather than too little. If the dough is dry and crumbly, the filling is likely to seep through the bottom crust, even when there are no visible cracks or holes. When you divide the finished dough before wrapping and chilling, allow a slightly larger portion for the bottom crust than for the top. The bottom crust needs to be rolled a tad thick to withstand the juices released by the fruit during baking.

Forming a Covered Fruit Pie

Roll out the bottom crust, fit it into the pan, and trim the overhanging dough to ¾ inch all around (see *How to Roll Out Pastry Dough*, 19). Patch any holes, tears, or thin spots with dough scraps, dabbing them on one side with cold water and then firmly pressing them, moistened side down, into place. Cover any short spots in the overhang in the same manner; if the pie is to be well sealed, you must have a wide overhang all around. Carefully transfer the lined pan to the refrigerator. Roll the remaining half of the dough into a 12-inch round, slip a rimless cookie sheet beneath it, and refrigerate it. (To make a plain or woven lattice top, see *How to Make a Lattice Top*, 41.)

Prepare the filling as your recipe directs. Remove the bottom crust from the refrigerator and fill it. Dot the top with butter if your recipe calls for it. Brush the overhanging edge of the bottom crust with cold water and place the top crust over the pie. Firmly pinch the edges of both crusts together with your fingers to seal. Trim the doubled edge to make an even overhang of ¾ inch, then tuck the overhang underneath itself (**1**) so that the folded edge is flush with the rim of the pie pan.

Crimp or flute the edge as for a single-crust pie (see page 21); a high fluted rim will help to contain any juices that bubble through the top crust. Cut three or four 2-inch slashes in the top crust (**2**) to allow steam to escape during baking.

If you wish, cut scraps of dough into decorative shapes, brush lightly with cold water, and press onto the top crust (**3**).

Baking the Pie

Fruit pies must be baked as soon as they are filled and assembled, or the juicy filling will begin to soften the bottom crust. Thoroughly preheat the oven and place the pie on the lowest oven rack to brown and crisp the undercrust and prevent the upper crust from becoming too dark. Fruit pies made with raw fillings are baked at a high temperature for 30 minutes to set the crust, then baked about 30 minutes more at a moderate temperature to cook the filling. Pies made with precooked fillings are baked at a high temperature throughout, generally for somewhat less time than for raw fruit fillings. The downfall of untold fruit pies is a flabby, underbaked crust.

Do not declare the pie done until the top has turned a deep, rich brown, almost the color of a hazelnut shell, and thick juices bubble enthusiastically through the steam vents or lattice. Remember that pies glazed with egg, milk, or cream will often brown within the first 30 minutes of baking, long before they are baked through. You can slow, though not stop, the browning process by laying a sheet of aluminum foil loosely over the top crust. Fruit pies are apt to char around the edge, especially when the pies spill over. Do not worry. A charred rim is a small price to pay for a well-baked crust.

Making a Pie with Any Fruit

One 9-inch pie; 6 to 8 servings

Once you develop a feel for making fruit pies, you can virtually dispense with recipes. A 9-inch pie (opposite) needs about 5 cups of fresh fruit or berries plus sugar, thickener, and a little butter. You will seldom go wrong if you use the formula below. There are, of course, special cases. Tart fruits such as sour cherries, rhubarb, cranberries, gooseberries, blackberries, fresh currants, and green tomatoes require 1 to 1½ cups sugar. Apples need only half as much thickener, while juicy berries may require one-third more, especially if they are heavily sweetened.

5 cups sliced fruit, peeled if necessary, or berries
¾ cup sugar
3 tablespoons quick-cooking tapioca or cornstarch

1 tablespoon strained fresh lemon juice
⅛ teaspoon salt
2 to 3 tablespoons unsalted butter, cut into small pieces

Mix the fruit, sugar, thickener, lemon juice, and salt and let stand for 15 minutes before pouring it into the pie crust. Dot the butter over the filling. Brush the edge of the bottom crust with cold water, then cover with the top crust or lattice. Seal the edge, trim, and crimp or flute. Cut steam vents in the top crust.

Bake the pie in the lower third of a 425°F oven for 30 minutes; then slip a baking sheet beneath it, reduce the oven temperature to 350°F, and bake the pie until thick juices bubble through the vents, about 30 minutes more.

Apple Pie I

One 9-inch pie; 6 to 8 servings

We like using Golden Delicious apples in this pie because they retain their texture and do not flood the pie with juice. Gala and Fuji are also good. Classic alternatives are: Newton Pippin, Rhode Island Greening, Winesap, Northern Spy, and Jonathan. We do not recommend Granny Smiths; although crisp when raw, all too often they turn mushy when baked in a pie with both a top and a bottom crust. Apple pie is best with a rich crust. A lard crust is superb; an ordinary flaky pastry crust made entirely with vegetable shortening makes a surprisingly close facsimile. Deluxe Butter Flaky Pastry Dough, 17, is also very good. Because the filling starts out heaped, a lattice top is not feasible; if you want a lattice, make Apple Pie II, 40, in which the filling is partially cooked before going into the pie. It is crucial to slice the apples about ¼ inch thick, measured at the thicker end. If the apple slices are thinner, the filling is apt to turn mushy; if thicker, the pie will not hold together when it is cut. Resist the temptation to add other spices or flavorings. A hint of cinnamon is all that is needed. Before beginning, please read the material on pages 34 to 35, and Apples, right.

Prepare:

Flaky Pastry Dough, 15, Lard Flaky Pastry Dough, 15, or Deluxe Butter Flaky Pastry Dough, 17

Roll half the dough into a 13-inch round, fit it into a 9-inch pie pan, and trim the overhanging dough to ¾ inch all around. Refrigerate. Roll the other half of the dough into a 12-inch round for the top crust and refrigerate it.

Position a rack in the lower third of the oven. Preheat the oven to 425°F. Peel, core, and slice ¼ inch thick:

2½ pounds apples (5 to 6 medium-large)

Measure 6 cups. Combine the apples with:

¾ cup sugar

2 to 3 tablespoons all-purpose flour

1 tablespoon strained fresh lemon juice (optional)

½ teaspoon ground cinnamon

⅛ teaspoon salt

Let stand for 15 minutes, stirring several times, so that the apples soften slightly and will better fit into the crust. Pour the mixture into the bottom crust and gently level with the back of a spoon. Dot the top with:

2 tablespoons unsalted butter, cut into small pieces

Brush the edge of the bottom crust with cold water. Cover with the top crust, then seal the edge, trim, and crimp or flute. Cut steam vents and sprinkle with:

2 teaspoons sugar

⅛ teaspoon ground cinnamon

Bake the pie for 30 minutes. Slip a baking sheet beneath it, reduce the oven temperature to 350°F, and bake until the fruit feels just tender when a knife or skewer is poked through a steam vent and thick juices have begun to bubble through the vents, 30 to 45 minutes more. For the filling to thicken properly, the pie must cool completely on a rack, 3 to 4 hours. If you wish to serve the pie warm, place it in a 350°F oven for about 15 minutes. The pie is best the day it is baked, but it can be kept for 2 to 3 days at room temperature.

APPLES

Apples are classed according to how they are used. *Eating* apples are, as a rule, crisp or crunchy, juicy, sweet or sweet-tart, with an intriguing aroma and complex flavor. *Cooking* apples are usually firmer and on the tart side, although they may be juicy and touched with sweetness. Most apples contain between 10 and 14 percent sugar. Tart apples just contain more malic acid, which blunts their sweetness. The texture of an apple's cooked flesh can be fluffy, as in a baked Rome Beauty; tender but intact, as in a Jonagold; or thick, as in Newton Pippin applesauce. A few splendid varieties like Golden Delicious and Gravenstein are suited to both eating and cooking.

When buying apples, look for fruit with flesh that feels firm and tight beneath the skin. There should be no soft spots, dark bruises, or holes. Do not be deceived by size. Larger apples tend to mature faster and thus can be mealier than small ones. For fast ripening, keep apples at room temperature. For longest keeping, refrigerate sound apples in perforated plastic bags or keep in a dry, cold place—32°F to 40°F. Mellow the flavor of cooking apples by leaving them at room temperature for a day or two before using.

To peel an apple, use a swivel-bladed vegetable peeler—a knife takes too much flesh.

Apple Pie II

One 9-inch pie; 6 to 8 servings

Because raw apples shrink a great deal during baking, apple pies tend to develop a gap between the top crust and fruit, causing the top crust to crumble when the pie is sliced. In this recipe, the filling is precooked and thus preshrunk, eliminating the gap and producing a beautifully full, compact pie that slices like a charm. Precooking also allows you to cover the pie with a lattice top if you choose. This pie is slightly softer than one made with raw apples. On the other hand, since the filling requires no thickener, the pie has a lovely fruity taste. To select apples for a pie, see page 38. Before beginning, please read the material on pages 34 to 35.
Prepare:

Flaky Pastry Dough, 15, Lard Flaky Pastry Dough, 15, or Deluxe Butter Flaky Pastry Dough, 17

Roll half the dough into a 13-inch round, fit it into a 9-inch pie pan, and trim the overhanging dough to ¾ inch all around. Refrigerate. Roll the other half into a 12-inch round for the top crust and refrigerate it. For a lattice top, see opposite. Peel, core, and slice a little thicker than ¼ inch:

3 pounds apples (about 6 large)

Measure 7 cups. In a very wide skillet or pot, heat over high heat until sizzling and fragrant:

3 tablespoons unsalted butter

Add the apples and toss until glazed with the butter. Reduce the heat to medium, cover tightly, and cook, stirring frequently, until the apples are softened but still slightly crunchy, 5 to 7 minutes. Stir in:

¾ cup sugar

½ teaspoon ground cinnamon

⅛ teaspoon salt

Increase the heat to high and, stirring to prevent scorching, cook the apples at a rapid boil until the juices become thick and syrupy, about 3 minutes. Immediately spread the apples in a thin layer on a baking sheet and let them cool. Position a rack in the lower third of the oven. Preheat the oven to 425°F. Pour the apple mixture into the bottom crust. Brush the overhanging edge of the bottom crust with cold water. Cover with the top crust or lattice, then seal the edge, trim, and crimp or flute. If using a closed top crust, cut steam vents. Bake until the crust is richly browned and the filling has begun to bubble, 40 to 50 minutes. Let cool completely on a rack, 3 to 4 hours. If you wish to serve the pie warm, place it in a 350°F oven for about 15 minutes. The pie is best the day it is baked, but it can be kept at room temperature for 2 to 3 days.

Blueberry Pie

One 9-inch pie; 8 servings

If you are constructing a lattice, use cornstarch, and the greater amount suggested, to prevent a granular or watery filling from bubbling over the strips. Before beginning, please read the material on pages 34 to 35.
Prepare:

Flaky Pastry Dough, 15, Deluxe Butter Flaky Pastry Dough, 17, Cornmeal Flaky Pastry Dough, 17, or double recipe Flaky Cream Cheese Pastry Dough, 18

Roll half the dough into a 13-inch round, fit it into a 9-inch pie pan, and trim, leaving a ¾-inch overhang. Refrigerate. Roll the other half of the dough into a 12-inch round for the top crust and refrigerate it. For a lattice top, see opposite. Position a rack in the lower third of the oven. Preheat the oven to 425°F. Combine and let stand 15 minutes:

5 cups blueberries, picked over

¾ to 1 cup sugar

3½ to 4 tablespoons quick-cooking tapioca or cornstarch

1 tablespoon strained fresh lemon juice

1 teaspoon grated lemon zest (optional)

⅛ teaspoon salt

Pour the mixture into the bottom crust and dot with:

1 to 2 tablespoons unsalted butter, cut into small pieces

Brush the edge of the bottom crust with cold water. Cover with the top crust or lattice, then seal the edge, trim, and crimp or flute. If using a closed top crust, cut steam vents. Bake the pie for 30 minutes. Slip a baking sheet beneath it, reduce the oven temperature to 350°F, and bake until thick juices bubble through the vents, 25 to 35 minutes more. Let cool. The pie is best the day it is baked, but it can be stored at room temperature for up to 1 day.

HOW TO MAKE A LATTICE TOP

Lattice tops are fun to make. A plain lattice, which simply entails laying strips of dough in a crisscross pattern over the top of the pie, requires less patience than a woven lattice, but both are easy. To measure and cut the strips, you will need a ruler and a small, sharp knife. A decorative pastry wheel (pastry jagger) will put a pretty edge on the strips, but this tool is not necessary. To pick up and move the strips, a metal dough scraper is helpful but, again, not essential.

Woven lattices tend to soften and become juice-soaked when formed directly on the pie, so construct them on a cookie sheet and then transfer them, chilled, to the pie. Since tapioca granules that are exposed in the spaces of a lattice sometimes fail to soften, it is wise to thicken fillings for lattice-top pies with cornstarch (or flour) instead.

1 *To Form a Plain Lattice Top:* For a 9-inch pie pan, roll the dough reserved for the top crust into a 13½-inch round and trim the round to make a 10-inch square. Cut the square of dough into 18 strips, each about ½ inch wide. Spoon the filling into the bottom crust of the pie and brush the edge of the bottom crust with cold water. Place 9 of the dough strips ½ inch apart on top of the pie, then arrange the remaining dough strips over these, either on a diagonal or in a perpendicular criss-cross pattern.

2 Trim the lattice strips so that they hang over the edge of the bottom crust at least ¼ inch on each end. Press the strips against the bottom

crust. Fold the edge of the bottom crust up, covering the ends of the lattice strips, then crimp or flute the edge.

3 *To Form a Woven Lattice Top:* For a 9-inch pie pan, roll the dough reserved for the top crust into a 13½-inch round and trim the round to make a 10-inch square. Cut the square into eighteen ½-inch strips. Arrange 9 of the strips ½ inch apart on a floured rimless cookie sheet (or on the back of a baking pan). Fold every other strip halfway back, making the ends meet, then place 1 strip crosswise just beyond the folded edge. Return the folded strips to their original flat position over the perpendicular strip. Fold back the strips that you just left flat and then place a second strip cross-wise just beyond the folded edge. Unfold strips over the second per-pendicular strip. Repeat until you have woven 5 crosswise strips into the lattice, completing one half. Now weave the remaining 4 cross-wise strips into the lattice starting on the other side of the center crosswise strip, completing the other half. Refrigerate the lattice until firm.

4 Fill the bottom crust of the pie and brush the exposed edge with cold water. Slide the lattice off the sheet onto the pie. Trim the lattice strips so that they hang over the edge of the bottom crust at least ¼ inch on each end. Press the strips against the bottom crust. Fold the edge of the bottom crust up, covering the ends of the lattice strips, then crimp or flute the edge.

Cherry Pie

One 9-inch pie; 8 servings

Sour cherries make the best pie. They are tastier after cooking, since they are highly acidic and heat helps them absorb sweeteners. In lieu of sour cherries, use ripe Bing cherries. A cherry or olive pitter, a device that looks like a paper punch, is a welcome time-saver here. Before beginning, please read the material on pages 34 to 35.

Prepare:

Flaky Pastry Dough, 15, Lard Flaky Pastry Dough, 15, Deluxe Butter Flaky Pastry Dough, 17, or double recipe Flaky Cream Cheese Pastry Dough, 18

Roll half the dough into a 13-inch round, fit it into a 9-inch pie pan, and trim the overhanging dough to ¾ inch all around. Refrigerate. Roll the other half into a 12-inch round for the top crust and refrigerate it. For a lattice top, see page 41. Position a rack in the lower third of the oven. Preheat the oven to 425°F. Combine and let stand for 15 minutes:

5 cups pitted sour or Bing cherries (2 to 2½ pounds)

1¼ cups sugar for sour cherries, or ¾ cup sugar for Bing cherries

3 to 3½ tablespoons quick-cooking tapioca or cornstarch (use the greater amount of cornstarch for a lattice pie)

2 tablespoons water

1 tablespoon strained fresh lemon juice

¼ teaspoon almond extract

1 to 2 drops red food coloring (optional)

Pour the mixture into the bottom crust and dot with:

2 to 3 tablespoons unsalted butter, cut into small pieces

Brush the overhanging edge of the bottom crust with cold water. Cover with the top crust or lattice, then seal the edge, trim, and crimp or flute. If using a closed top crust, cut steam vents. Bake the pie for 30 minutes. Slip a baking sheet beneath it, reduce the oven temperature to 350°F, and bake until thick juices bubble through the vents, 25 to 35 minutes more. Let cool completely on a rack before serving. Store at room temperature for up to 1 day.

SOUR CHERRIES

Although most commercial sour cherries, also called pie or tart cherries, are canned, you may find fresh morellos, delightful with their red juice, or amarelles, with their clear juice, close to where they are grown. Sour cherries ripen a couple of weeks after sweet cherries. Montmorency, a morello, is the principal sour cherry in this country. It is predominantly grown in New England, around the Great Lakes, and on the Great Plains. Heart-shaped Duke cherries are a sweet-and-sour cross. Their sprightly yellow flesh is good for cooking and for preserves. Sour cherries are sent to market ripe. Choose them individually (never packaged) after tasting one for flavor. Select the largest, glossiest, plumpest, brightest, and firmest with the greenest stems.

Canned Fruit Pies

Canned fruits, preferably packed in unsweetened juice, make acceptable pies. For Cherry Pie with Canned or Bottled Fruit, *see opposite; for* Winter Peach Pie, *see page 47. Otherwise use the formula below.*

Prepare:

Flaky Pastry Dough, 15

Roll half of the dough into a 13-inch round, fit it into a 9-inch pie pan, and trim the overhanging dough to ¾ inch all around. Refrigerate. Roll the other half into a 12-inch round for the top crust and refrigerate it. If you wish to make a lattice top, see page 41.

Position a rack in the lower third of the oven. Preheat the oven to 425°F.

Pour into a sieve set over a bowl:

3 pounds canned fruit, such as sliced pears or peaches, halved apricots, chopped pineapple, or whole plums

Shake the fruit lightly to drain. Measure 3½ cups fruit and ½ cup juice and combine in a bowl with:

½ to ¾ cup sugar

3 tablespoons quick-cooking tapioca or cornstarch (use cornstarch for a lattice pie)

2 tablespoons strained fresh lemon juice

Let the mixture stand for 15 minutes, then pour into the bottom crust. If the crust seems too full to be covered with a pastry lid, remove

a little of the fruit and liquid. Dot with:

2 tablespoons unsalted butter, cut into small pieces

Brush the overhanging edge of the bottom crust with cold water. Cover with the top crust or lattice, then seal the edge, trim, and crimp or flute. If using a closed top crust, cut steam vents. Bake the pie for 30 minutes. Slip a baking sheet beneath the pan, reduce the oven temperature to 350°F, and bake until thick juices bubble through the vents, 25 to 35 minutes more. Let cool completely on a rack before serving.

Cherry Pie with Canned or Bottled Fruit

One 9-inch pie; 8 servings

Canned or bottled sour cherries make a more flavorful pie than canned or bottled sweet ones. Adjust the sugar depending on which type you have and the packing liquid used. Before beginning, please read the material on pages 34 to 35.

Prepare:

Flaky Pastry Dough, 15, Lard Flaky Pastry Dough, 15, Deluxe Butter Flaky Pastry Dough, 17, or double recipe Flaky Cream Cheese Pastry Dough, 18

Roll half the dough into a 13-inch round, fit it into a 9-inch pie pan, and trim the overhanging dough to ¾ inch all around. Refrigerate. Roll the other half into a 12-inch round for the top crust and refrigerate it. For a lattice top, see page 41.

Position a rack in the lower third of the oven. Preheat the oven to 425°F. Pour into a sieve set over a bowl:

3 pounds bottled or canned, pitted cherries

Shake the cherries lightly to drain. Measure 4 cups fruit and ½ cup juice and combine with:

½ cup sugar for sweet cherries in syrup, ¾ cup sugar for sour cherries in light syrup, or 1¼ cups sugar for sour cherries packed in water

3 tablespoons quick-cooking tapioca or cornstarch (use cornstarch for a lattice pie)

1 tablespoon strained fresh lemon juice

¼ teaspoon almond extract

Let stand for 15 minutes, then pour into the bottom crust and dot with:

2 to 3 tablespoons butter, cut into small pieces

Brush the overhanging edge of the bottom crust with cold water. Cover with the top crust or lattice, then seal the edge, trim, and crimp or flute. If using a closed top crust, cut steam vents. Bake the pie for 30 minutes. Slip a baking sheet beneath it, reduce the oven temperature to 350°F, and bake until thick juices bubble through the vents, 25 to 35 minutes more. Let cool completely on a rack before serving. Store at room temperature for up to 1 day.

FREEZING FRUIT PIES

Fruit pies, except those made with custard, freeze surprisingly well. For best results, freeze the pies before baking. Form the pie in a pan lined with plastic wrap. Do not cut steam vents in the top or apply a glaze. Freeze the pie solid, then pry it out of the pan and peel off the wrap. Wrap the pie airtight in foil, seal it in a plastic bag, and freeze for up to 6 months. When you are ready to bake the pie, return it, still frozen but unwrapped, to its original pan and glaze it if you wish. Bake the pie at 425°F for 10 minutes, cut vents in the top, and bake for 20 minutes more. Reduce the oven temperature to 350°F and bake the pie until thick juices bubble through the vents, about 1 hour longer.

Peach Pie

One 9-inch pie; 8 servings

Whether freestone or clingstone, yellow or white, peaches make a luscious pie. Before beginning, please read the material on pages 34 to 35. For tips on peeling peaches, see page 65.
Prepare:
Flaky Pastry Dough, 15, Lard Flaky Pastry Dough, 15, Deluxe Butter Flaky Pastry Dough, 17, or double recipe Flaky Cream Cheese Pastry Dough, 18
Roll half the dough into a 13-inch round, fit it into a 9-inch pie pan and trim the overhanging dough to ¾ inch all around. Refrigerate. Roll the other half into a 12-inch round for the top crust and refrigerate it. For a lattice top, see page 41. Position a rack in the lower third of the oven. Preheat the oven to 425°F.

Peel, pit, and slice ¼ inch thick:
2½ pounds peaches
Measure 5 cups and combine with:
½ to ¾ cup sugar
3 to 3½ tablespoons quick-cooking tapioca or cornstarch (use the greater amount of cornstarch for a lattice pie)
3 tablespoons strained fresh lemon juice
¼ teaspoon almond extract (optional)
⅛ teaspoon salt
Let stand for 15 minutes, stirring occasionally. Pour into the bottom crust and dot with:
2 to 3 tablespoons unsalted butter, cut into small pieces
Brush the overhanging edge of the

bottom crust with cold water. Cover with the top crust or lattice, then seal the edge, trim, and crimp or flute. If using a closed top crust, cut steam vents. Lightly brush the top of the pie with:
Milk or cream
Sprinkle with:
2 teaspoons sugar
Bake the pie for 30 minutes. Slip a baking sheet beneath it, reduce the oven temperature to 350°F, and bake until thick juices bubble through the vents, 25 to 35 minutes more. Let cool completely on a rack before serving. This pie (opposite) is best the day it is baked, but it can be stored at room temperature for up to 1 day.

Winter Peach Pie

One 9-inch pie; 8 servings

This pie can also be made in the summer with 5 cups sliced fresh peaches in place of the canned. It is gorgeous with a lattice top. Before beginning, please read the material on pages 34 to 35.
Prepare:
Flaky Pastry Dough, 15, Lard Flaky Pastry Dough, 15, Deluxe Butter Flaky Pastry Dough, 17, or double recipe Flaky Cream Cheese Pastry Dough, 18
Roll half the dough into a 13-inch round, fit it into a 9-inch pie pan, and trim the overhanging dough to ¾ inch all around. Refrigerate. Roll the other half into a 12-inch round for the top crust and refrigerate it. For a lattice top, see page 41. Position a rack in the lower third of the oven. Preheat the oven to 425°F. Pour into a sieve set over a bowl:

2½ pounds canned sliced peaches, packed in juice
Shake the peaches lightly to drain. Measure 3 cups fruit and ½ cup juice and combine with:
⅔ cup dark raisins
⅔ cup firmly packed light brown sugar
3 tablespoons quick-cooking tapioca or cornstarch (use cornstarch for a lattice pie)
2 tablespoons strained fresh lemon juice
½ teaspoon ground ginger
¼ teaspoon ground cinnamon
¼ teaspoon ground mace or freshly grated or ground nutmeg
⅛ teaspoon ground cloves
Let stand for 15 minutes, then pour into the bottom crust and dot with:

2 to 3 tablespoons unsalted butter, cut into small pieces
Brush the overhanging edge of the bottom crust with cold water. Cover with the top crust or lattice, then seal the edge, trim, and crimp or flute. If using a closed top crust, cut steam vents. Whisk together, then lightly brush the top of the pie with:
1 large egg yolk
⅛ teaspoon water
Bake the pie for 30 minutes. Slip a baking sheet beneath it, reduce the oven temperature to 350°F, and bake until thick juices bubble through the vents, 25 to 35 minutes more. Let cool completely on a rack before serving. Store at room temperature for up to 1 day.

Combination Fillings

Fruit pies filled with combinations of fruits and berries are infinite in possibility and often magical in result. However, those who demand predictability should not venture out onto this limb. It is tricky to gauge the thickening and sweetening required for combination fillings, and the colors are sometimes startling. We recommend the following combinations:

3½ cups sliced peeled pears and 1½ cups raspberries, cranberries, or dark raisins

3½ cups sliced peeled peaches and 1½ cups blueberries or raspberries

3 cups sliced peeled apples and 2 cups sliced green tomatoes

3½ cups sliced peeled apples and 1½ cups raspberries, blackberries, or fresh currants

2½ cups pitted sour cherries and 2½ cups diced rhubarb

4 cups pitted sour or sweet cherries and 1 cup dark raisins

2½ cups sliced strawberries and 2½ cups gooseberries

4 cups diced fresh pineapple and 1 cup dark raisins or sliced strawberries

2½ cups sliced bananas and 2½ cups blueberries or sliced strawberries

Rhubarb Pie

One 9-inch pie; 8 servings

If possible, make this pie early in the season, when the stalks are still thin skinned, pink, and no thicker than your thumb. Only mature rhubarb will require the greater amount of sugar suggested. Before beginning, please read the material on pages 34 to 35.

Prepare:

Flaky Pastry Dough, 15, Lard Flaky Pastry Dough, 15, Deluxe Butter Flaky Pastry Dough, 17, or double recipe Flaky Cream Cheese Pastry Dough, 18

Roll half the dough into a 13-inch round, fit it into a 9-inch pie pan, and trim the overhanging dough to ¾ inch all around. Refrigerate. Roll the other half into a 12-inch round for the top crust and refrigerate it. For a lattice top, see page 41. Position a rack in the lower third of the oven. Preheat the oven to 425°F. Cut into 1-inch lengths:

1¾ to 2 pounds rhubarb stalks

Measure 5 cups and combine with:

1¼ to 1½ cups sugar

¼ cup quick-cooking tapioca or cornstarch (use cornstarch for a lattice pie)

Grated zest of 1 orange (optional)

¼ teaspoon salt

Let stand for 15 minutes, stirring occasionally. Pour into the bottom crust and dot with:

2 tablespoons unsalted butter, cut into small pieces

Brush the overhanging edge of the bottom crust with cold water. Cover with the top crust or lattice, then seal the edge, trim, and crimp or flute. If using a closed top crust, cut steam vents. Lightly brush the top of the pie with:

Milk or cream

Sprinkle with:

2 teaspoons sugar

Bake the pie for 30 minutes. Slip a baking sheet beneath it, reduce the oven temperature to 350°F, and bake until thick juices bubble through the vents, 25 to 35 minutes more. Let cool completely on a rack before serving. This pie is best eaten the day it is baked, but it can be stored at room temperature for up to 1 day.

STRAWBERRY RHUBARB PIE

This pie (opposite) tastes more of strawberries than of rhubarb. Prepare Rhubarb Pie, left, substituting 2½ cups strawberries, hulled and halved lengthwise, for 2½ cups of the rhubarb. Decrease the sugar to 1 cup and omit the orange zest.

Raisin Pie

One 9-inch pie; 8 servings

Some raisin pies are made with cream, sour cream, and eggs and are similar to cream or chess pies. This one consists almost entirely of raisins. You can substitute dried sour cherries for up to half of the raisins. Before beginning, please read the material on pages 34 to 35.
Prepare:

Flaky Pastry Dough, 15, Lard Flaky Pastry Dough, 15, Deluxe Butter Flaky Pastry Dough, 17, or double recipe Flaky Cream Cheese Pastry Dough, 18

Roll half of the dough into a 13-inch round, fit it into a 9-inch pie pan, and trim the overhanging dough to ¾ inch all around. Refrigerate. Roll the other half of the dough into a 12-inch round for the top crust and refrigerate it. For a lattice top, see page 41.
Bring to a boil in a medium saucepan over high heat:

4 cups (1½ pounds) dark raisins, or 2 cups dark raisins and 2 cups golden raisins

2½ cups water

Reduce the heat and gently simmer for 5 minutes. Remove the saucepan from the heat. Mix thoroughly, then stir into the raisins:

1 cup firmly packed light or dark brown sugar

¼ cup all-purpose flour

¾ teaspoon ground cinnamon (optional)

½ teaspoon salt

Add:

3 tablespoons unsalted butter, cut into bits

1 tablespoon strained fresh lemon juice or any kind of vinegar

Bring to a simmer over medium heat, stirring constantly, then continue to simmer for 1 minute. Let cool to room temperature.
Position a rack in the center of the oven. Preheat the oven to 400°F. Turn the filling into the bottom crust. Brush the overhanging bottom crust with cold water. Cover with the top crust or lattice, then seal the edge, trim, and crimp or flute. If using a closed top crust, cut steam vents. If you wish, brush the top of the pie with:

1 large egg yolk beaten with ⅛ teaspoon water

Bake the pie until the crust is richly browned and the filling is bubbly, 40 to 45 minutes. Let cool completely on a rack. Store at room temperature for up to 2 days.
Accompany with:

Whipped Cream, 76, or vanilla ice cream

RAISINS

Raisins, which, of course, are simply dried grapes, are classified as seedless, which grow without seeds, and seeded, which have had the seeds removed. Dark seedless raisins are sun-dried principally from green Thompson Seedless grapes, the same ones we buy at the market. Monukka raisins are made from large green grapes with a richer flavor than Thompson. Golden seedless raisins are also Thompsons but have been oven-dried and treated with sulfur dioxide. Sultanas are also golden, sweet, and seedless but are dried from a yellow-green Turkish grape. They are the standard pale raisin abroad and sometimes can be found in fancy groceries.

Concord Grape Pie

One 9-inch pie; 8 servings

Use only Concord grapes or a related variety whose skins slip off when pinched. Before beginning, please read the material on pages 34 to 35.

Prepare:

Flaky Pastry Dough, 15, or Deluxe Butter Flaky Pastry Dough, 17

Roll half of the dough into a 13-inch round, fit it into a 9-inch pie pan, and trim the overhanging dough to ¾ inch all around. Refrigerate. Roll the other half of the dough into a 12-inch round for the top crust and refrigerate it. For a lattice top, see page 41.

Rinse, stem, and pick over:

4 cups Concord grapes (about 2 pounds)

One at a time, pinch the grapes to slip off the skins, reserving both skins and pulp. Simmer the pulp in a saucepan over medium heat until the seeds loosen, about 5 minutes. Strain through a coarse sieve into a bowl and discard the seeds. Add the skins to the pulp, then whisk in:

¾ to 1 cup sugar

2 tablespoons unsalted butter, cut into bits

1 tablespoon strained fresh lemon juice

⅛ teaspoon salt

Let cool, then whisk in:

2½ to 3 tablespoons quick-cooking tapioca or cornstarch (use the greater amount of cornstarch for a lattice pie)

Position a rack in the lower third of the oven. Preheat the oven to 425°F. Turn the filling into the bottom crust. Brush the overhanging edge of the bottom crust with cold water. Cover with top crust or lattice, then seal the edge, trim, and crimp or flute. If using a closed top crust, cut steam vents. If you wish, brush the top of the pie with:

1 large egg yolk beaten with ⅛ teaspoon water

And sprinkle with:

2 teaspoons sugar (optional)

Bake the pie for 30 minutes. Slip a baking sheet beneath it, reduce the oven temperature to 350°F, and bake until thick juices bubble through the vents, 25 to 35 minutes longer. Let cool completely on a rack. The pie can be stored at room temperature for up to 1 day.

GRAPES

Grapes native to this country have comparatively thicker skin that slips easily from the pulp—they are often called slipskins—than those from abroad. Fox grapes, native from New England to Georgia to Indiana, are the principal American species. Foxes may be sweet but are usually astringent, with a spicy musky aroma and a flavor that has come to be described as "foxy." Concords—the grapes of commercial jelly and purple juice—are a superlative example of fox grapes.

Fillings with Frozen Fruit

If you buy frozen fruits such as peaches, cherries, or berries, choose those that are "individually frozen" or "dry-packed," meaning that they have been processed without sugar and come in loose pieces rather than a block.

Follow any recipe calling for fresh fruit, substituting an equal volume of frozen fruit. Since frozen fruit resists settling in the cup, it must be measured by a special procedure. Separate the pieces and knock off clinging ice, but do not thaw. Pour the fruit into a 4-cup measure, shake to settle it as much as possible, and measure 4 level cups. Measure out 1 more cup in a 1-cup measure. Toss the still-frozen fruit with the other ingredients, using the maximum amount of thickening called for, and spoon the filling into the crust at once, without the usual 15-minute standing time. If the fruit is allowed to thaw, it will release a flood of juice and make the crust soggy. Do not glaze the top crust with sugar or egg. Bake the pie at 400°F for 50 minutes; then slip a baking sheet beneath it and bake at 350°F until thick juices bubble through the vents, 25 to 40 minutes more.

Deep-Dish Fruit Pies

Deep-dish pies are simply covered fruit pies baked without a bottom crust. Despite their name, these pies should be baked in dishes that are relatively wide and shallow rather than narrow and deep, so that there is enough crust in relation to fruit. The 10-inch Pyrex dishes made expressly for deep-dish pies—they lack the flared rim of ordinary pie pans—are serviceable for recipes made with up to 6 cups fruit. For pies with more generous fillings, choose a glass or ceramic casserole.

Any fruit pie in this chapter can be baked as a deep-dish pie. Since the filling need not be firm enough to slice—deep-dish pies are served with a spoon—you can decrease the thickening by up to half. For the top crust, use a half recipe of any flaky pastry dough, 15 to 17, or a full recipe of *Flaky Cream Cheese Pastry Dough*, 18. Roll the dough the same shape as, but a little wider than, the top of the dish, lay it over the filling, and tuck the edges against the inside of the dish. Cut steam vents in the top. If you wish, sprinkle the crust with sugar or glaze with an egg yolk beaten with ⅛ teaspoon water. Set the pie on a baking sheet and bake in the center of a preheated 375°F oven until the crust is nicely browned and juices bubble through the vents, about 1 hour.

Deep-Dish Apple Pie with Cheddar Crust

One 9-inch pie; 8 servings

Combine and toss together:
¾ cup lightly packed grated extra-sharp Cheddar cheese
⅔ cup all-purpose flour
6 tablespoons cold unsalted butter, cut into ¼-inch pieces
Chop the mixture with a pastry blender to the consistency of coarse crumbs, then press together with your fingers and knead in the bowl until a cohesive dough forms. Flatten the dough into a 4-inch disk, wrap in plastic, and refrigerate until firm but malleable, 30 to 60 minutes. Flour the dough lightly, then roll into a 9-inch round between sheets of wax paper. Slip a rimless cookie sheet beneath the dough and refrigerate until firm, about 30 minutes.

Position a rack in the center of the oven. Preheat the oven to 375°F. Heat over high heat in a very wide skillet (not cast iron) until sizzling and fragrant:
6 tablespoons (¾ stick) unsalted butter
Add:
2 pounds Golden Delicious, Gala, Fuji, or Newton Pippin apples (about 4 medium-large) peeled, cored, and sliced ¼ inch thick
Toss with a wooden spoon until the apples release their juice and are tender, 5 to 7 minutes; reduce the heat if the apples begin to color. Stir in:
1 cup dark raisins (optional)
½ cup chopped walnuts or pecans
½ cup sugar
Grated zest of 1 large lemon
Strained juice of 1 large lemon
¼ cup brandy (optional)
½ teaspoon salt
½ teaspoon freshly grated or ground nutmeg
¼ teaspoon ground cinnamon
¼ teaspoon ground cloves
Boil over high heat, stirring occasionally, until the juices thicken to the consistency of maple syrup. Pour the mixture into a 9-inch pie pan. Peel the top sheet of wax paper off the dough, then flip the dough onto the filling and peel off the bottom sheet. Let the dough soften slightly, then tuck the edges inside the rim of the pan and cut two 2-inch steam vents. Place the pie on a baking sheet and bake until the crust is golden brown and the filling is bubbly, 30 to 40 minutes. Let cool slightly before serving. The pie can be made up to 12 hours ahead and warmed in a 350°F oven for 10 to 15 minutes. Accompany with:
Vanilla ice cream

Deep-Dish Pear Pie with Cranberries and Apples

One 10- to 12-inch pie; 8 to 10 servings

Prepare:

½ recipe Flaky Pastry Dough, 15 or Deluxe Butter Flaky Pastry Dough, 17

Position a rack in the center of the oven. Preheat the oven to 375°F. In a 10- to 12-inch (2½ quart) deep-dish pie pan, combine:

3½ pounds firm ripe pears (about 7 large), peeled, cored, and cut into ¼-inch-thick slices

1½ pounds firm tart apples (about 3 large), peeled, cored, and cut into ⅛-inch-thick slices

2½ cups (8 ounces) cranberries, picked over

1⅓ cups sugar

⅓ cup all-purpose flour

1 tablespoon strained fresh lemon juice

⅛ teaspoon salt

Stir gently until well blended. If you wish, dot the top with:

2 to 4 tablespoons unsalted butter, cut into small pieces

Roll the dough to fit the top of the dish, lay it over the filling, and tuck in the edges. Cut 3 or 4 steam vents in the crust. Brush the top with:

2 tablespoons beaten egg (½ large)

Place the pie on a baking sheet and bake until the crust is golden brown and juices bubble through the vents, about 1 hour. Let cool on a rack. The pie can be stored at room temperature for up to 1 day. Serve warm or at room temperature with:

Vanilla ice cream

Mince Pie

Mince pie dates back to medieval English baking and came to America with the first settlers. Until the late nineteenth century, Americans considered it the choicest of all pies—an obligatory dessert at Thanksgiving and Christmas. Originally, the central ingredient was minced or finely chopped meat, usually beef but sometimes veal or venison—hence the name. In our grandmother's day, meatless mince pies were still the exception rather than the norm, but most contemporary versions do not contain meat.

Mince Pie

One 9-inch pie; 8 servings

A handsome pie with a delicious flavor quite unlike that of commercial mincemeats. Before beginning, please read the material on pages 34 to 35.
Prepare:
Flaky Pastry Dough, 15, or Deluxe Butter Flaky Pastry Dough, 17
Roll half the dough into a 13-inch round, fit it into a 9-inch pie pan, and trim the overhanging dough to ¾ inch all around. Refrigerate. Roll the other half into a 12-inch round for the top crust and refrigerate it. For a lattice top, see page 41.
Combine in a medium, heavy pot or saucepan:
3 medium-large Golden Delicious apples, peeled, cored, and cut into ¾-inch chunks
1½ cups dark raisins, coarsely chopped
1 cup walnuts or pecans, coarsely chopped
1 cup sugar
¼ cup apple juice or cider
¼ cup brandy or apple juice
4 tablespoons (½ stick) unsalted butter
Grated zest of ½ lemon
Strained juice of ½ lemon
1 tablespoon cider vinegar
1 teaspoon salt
1 teaspoon ground cinnamon
½ teaspoon freshly grated or ground nutmeg
¼ teaspoon ground cloves
Bring to a boil over high heat. Reduce the heat to low and gently simmer, stirring frequently, until the bottom of the pot is almost dry and the fruits are glazed with a thick, molasses-like syrup, 20 to 30 minutes. Let cool to room temperature. Position a rack in the center of the oven. Preheat the oven to 400°F. Pour the filling into the bottom crust. Brush the overhanging edge of the bottom crust with cold water. Cover with the top crust or lattice, then seal the edge, trim, and crimp or flute. If using a closed top crust, cut steam vents. Whisk together, then brush the top of the pie with:
1 large egg yolk
⅛ teaspoon water
Bake the pie for 30 minutes. Reduce the oven temperature to 350°F and bake until the crust is richly browned, 30 to 40 minutes more. Let cool completely on a rack, then refrigerate for up to 1 week. Before serving, warm the pie in a 300°F oven for about 20 minutes. Serve with:
***Hard Sauce, right,* or vanilla ice cream**

Hard Sauce

About 2½ cups; 16 servings

When spooned onto the hot pie, part of the sauce melts, bathing the mincemeat in a warm, buttery glaze, while the rest remains a delightfully cool and creamy froth, like whipped cream.
Combine in a large bowl:
½ pound (2 sticks) unsalted butter, softened but cool
3 cups powdered sugar, sifted if lumpy
2 teaspoons vanilla
½ teaspoon freshly grated or ground nutmeg
Beat on high speed until light and fluffy but still thick enough to hold a firm shape, 6 to 10 minutes. Still beating, very slowly add:
¼ cup brandy, Cognac, dark rum, or fresh orange juice
Especially if you have opted for a nonalcoholic sauce, you may also wish to add:
Grated zest of 1 orange
Use at once or cover tightly and refrigerate for up to 3 days. Soften the cold sauce at room temperature until spreadable.

ABOUT
SINGLE-CRUST
FRUIT PIES & TARTS

If you have little experience in baking pies, try your hand at a single-crust pie or tart. Unlike covered fruit pies, which must be made from a rolled, flaky pastry dough, open fruit pies can be made with a simpler pat-in-the-pan dough.

Unless the fruit will be obscured by streusel, arrange it on the dough with as much care and precision as your patience and time allow. The result will be a pie or tart that beguiles the eye as well as the palate.

Tarte Tatin, 64

Fresh Fruit Pastry Cream Tart

One 9½- or 10-inch tart; 8 servings

A fresh fruit pastry cream tart consists of uncooked berries or thinly sliced fruit artfully arranged over a thin layer of pastry cream in a tart crust. Almost any berries and fruits will do, including raspberries, strawberries, blueberries, plums, peaches, nectarines, kiwis, and star fruits. Avoid only very juicy fruits such as melon, hard or crisp fruits such as apples and pears, and bananas, which blacken. You can bake the crust and prepare the pastry cream up to 2 days in advance, but do not assemble the tart until shortly before serving, lest the crust soften and the fruit wilt. Both flaky pastry and shortbread crusts are suitable. If you prefer the former, make the crust with Deluxe Butter Flaky Pastry Dough, 17, *or* Sweet Flaky Pastry Dough, 17.

Prepare in a 9½- or 10-inch two-piece tart pan, glazing with the egg yolk:

Baked Flaky Pastry Crust, 22, or Shortbread Crust, 28

Let cool completely. To moisture-proof the crust, brush over the bottom:

3 tablespoons currant, raspberry, or strawberry jelly, melted, or 1 tablespoon unsalted butter, softened

Refrigerate the shell for 10 minutes to set the glaze or butter.
Meanwhile, in a medium bowl, beat on high speed until thick and pale yellow, about 2 minutes:

2 tablespoons plus 2 teaspoons sugar
1 tablespoon all-purpose flour
1 tablespoon cornstarch
2 large egg yolks

Meanwhile, combine in a medium stainless-steel or enamel saucepan and bring to a simmer:

½ cup plus 2½ tablespoons milk
½ vanilla bean, split (optional)

Fish out the vanilla bean if you used it. Gradually pour about one-third of the hot milk into the egg mixture, stirring to combine. Scrape the egg mixture back into the pan and cook, whisking constantly and scraping the bottom and corners of the pan to prevent scorching, over low to medium heat until the custard is thickened and begins to bubble. Then continue to cook, whisking, for 45 to 60 seconds. Using a clean spatula, scrape the custard into a clean bowl. If you have not used the vanilla bean, stir in:

½ teaspoon vanilla

Cover the surface of the custard with a piece of wax or parchment paper to prevent a skin from forming. Let cool, then refrigerate for at least 1 hour before using.
Spread the pastry cream evenly over the crust and arrange over the cream in a single layer:

2 cups whole small berries, sliced strawberries, or thinly sliced fruit

If you wish, brush the fruit lightly with:

2 to 3 tablespoons jelly, melted

Otherwise, just before serving, dust the tart very lightly with:

Powdered sugar

If not serving immediately, store in the refrigerator for no longer than 6 hours.

FRESH FRUIT CREAM TARTLETS

Prepare Fresh Fruit Pastry Cream Tart, *above, substituting* Baked Flaky Pastry Tartlet Crusts, 23, *for the large tart shell. Depending on the exact size and shape of your tartlet shells, you may need slightly more or less glaze, pastry cream, and fruit. Sliced fruit that fits the tartlet shell in a single-layer pinwheel, such as peaches, makes an especially effective presentation.*

Fresh Strawberry Pie

One 9-inch pie; 8 servings

One of America's most popular desserts, this pie is filled with uncooked strawberries bound together with a thickened berry puree. This is only as good as the berries you start with. Red or black raspberries can also be used.

Prepare in a 9-inch pie pan:

Baked Flaky Pastry Crust, 22, Pat-in-the-Pan Butter Crust, 26, or Crumb Crust, 30, made with graham crackers or vanilla wafers

Pick over:

6 cups strawberries or red or black raspberries

Rinse, dry, and hull the strawberries; cut any very large ones in half. Do not rinse the raspberries. Measure 4 cups of berries and set aside. Puree the remaining 2 cups berries in a blender or food processor. Whisk together in a medium saucepan:

1 cup sugar

¼ cup cornstarch

⅛ teaspoon salt

Whisk in:

½ cup water

Stir in the pureed berries along with:

2 tablespoons strained fresh lemon juice

2 tablespoons unsalted butter, cut into small pieces

Bring the mixture to a simmer over medium-high heat, stirring constantly, and cook for 1 minute. Pour half of the reserved berries into the crust and spoon half of the hot berry mixture over them. Gently shake the pie pan to coat the berries evenly. Cover with the remaining berries, spoon the remaining hot berry mixture over them, and gently shake the pan as before. Refrigerate the pie for at least 4 hours to set. This pie is best served the day it is made. Serve with:

Whipped Cream, 76

Apricot Frangipane Tart

One 9½- or 10-inch tart; 8 servings

Fresh apricots make a spectacular tart filling, especially when paired with a rich almond custard.

Prepare in a 9½- or 10-inch two-piece tart pan, glazing with the egg yolk:

Baked Flaky Pastry Crust, 22, or Shortbread Crust, 28

Let cool completely.

Position a rack in the lower third of the oven. Preheat the oven to 350°F Spread on a baking sheet:

1 cup slivered blanched almonds

Toast the nuts, stirring once or twice, until golden, about 7 minutes. Let cool to room temperature, then coarsely chop. In a medium bowl, cream with the back of a wooden spoon until light and fluffy:

4 tablespoons (½ stick) unsalted butter, softened

⅓ cup sugar

⅛ teaspoon almond extract

Beat in thoroughly:

1 large egg, at room temperature

Stir in the nuts. Spread the mixture over the bottom of the tart crust. Pit and slice ¼ inch thick:

4 large or 6 medium apricots

Arrange the apricots in concentric circles over the nut mixture, overlapping the slices slightly. Brush with:

2 to 3 tablespoons strained warmed apricot jam

Bake the tart until the nut custard is set, 20 to 25 minutes. Let cool on a rack. Serve slightly warm or at room temperature. Store refrigerated for up to 1 day.

Pear Streusel Tart

One 9½- or 10-inch tart; 8 servings

Prepare in a 9½- or 10-inch tart pan, glazing with the egg yolk:

Baked Flaky Pastry Crust, 22, or Pat-in-the-Pan Butter Crust, 26

Let cool completely.

Position a rack in the center of the oven. Preheat the oven to 350°F. Peel, core, and slice ¼ inch thick:

1½ pounds firm ripe pears (about 3 medium-large), preferably Bosc or Anjou

Measure 3 cups pears and toss with:

⅓ cup sugar
2 tablespoons all-purpose flour

Distribute the pear mixture in the tart crust. Cover evenly with:

Streusel, below

Bake the tart until the pears feel tender when pierced with a fork, 40 to 50 minutes. Let cool completely on a rack. Serve the tart on the day it is made (opposite).

Raspberry Streusel Tart

One 9½- or 10-inch tart; 8 servings

You can make this tart with any summer berry or with a mixture of berries.
Prepare in a 9½- or 10-inch two-piece tart pan, glazing with the egg yolk:

Baked Flaky Pastry Crust, 22, or Shortbread Crust, 28

Let cool completely.

Position a rack in the center of the oven. Preheat the oven to 350°F. Stir together just until combined:

3 cups raspberries
½ cup sugar

2 tablespoons cornstarch
1 tablespoon strained fresh lemon juice

Distribute the raspberry mixture evenly in the tart crust. Sprinkle over the berries:

Streusel, below

Bake the tart until the streusel has browned and thick juices bubble up near the center, 45 to 60 minutes. Let cool completely on a rack. Serve the tart the day it is made.

PEARS

European pears—fragile when ripe but sturdy while green—are the ideal growers' fruit, since the pears must ripen off the tree. On the tree, the fruit turns mealy. Pears are available year-round, but their natural peak season is August through October. Sometimes you will find ripe pears at the market. A pear is ripe when it smells like a pear and gives to gentle pressure applied at the stem end. Because some pears will rot before they ripen, it is wise to select the ripest pears available. Examine pears carefully for bruises. Superficial scrapes and blemishes are not important, but avoid pears with dark or soft spots or any shriveling. For the most part (Anjou is an exception), yellow pears deepen from green to yellow as they ripen, but red pears are red before they are ripe. Bartlett, Comice, Concorde, and Seckel will ripen to melting softness, but serve Anjou, Bosc, and Red Clapp's Favorite, and cook Winter Nellis, while slightly crisp.

Streusel

About 2 cups

Blend with a fork or pulse in a food processor until the mixture resembles coarse crumbs:

⅔ cup all-purpose flour
⅔ cup finely chopped walnuts or pecans

⅔ cup sugar or packed light brown sugar, or a combination
5 tablespoons unsalted butter, melted
1 teaspoon ground cinnamon
¼ teaspoon salt

Tarte Tatin

8 servings

This classic French upside-down apple tart is named for the Tatin sisters, who served it at their hotel in the Loire Valley. The apples are cut in quarters and arranged in circles over the bottom of a cast-iron skillet containing sugar and melted butter. The apples are cooked on the stove over high heat until their juices begin to darken and then covered with a pastry crust and baked. When the tart is turned out of the skillet, the crust becomes a base for dazzling concentric circles of translucent, caramelized apples. Prepare tarte Tatin in any ovenproof, deep, heavy skillet measuring 7 to 8 inches across the bottom and 10 to 11 inches across the top. The filling does not react with cast iron, but you may find a cast-iron skillet cumbersome and heavy to flip when unmolding the tart. Pans made specially for tarte Tatin are available at some cookware stores.

Prepare:

½ recipe Deluxe Butter Flaky Pastry Dough, 17

Roll the dough into a 12-inch round, slip a rimless cookie sheet beneath it, and refrigerate.

Position a rack in the upper third of the oven. Preheat the oven to 375°F. Peel, core, and quarter lengthwise:

6 medium-large Golden Delicious apples (about 3 pounds)

Melt in the skillet chosen for the tart (see note, left):

8 tablespoons (1 stick) unsalted butter

Remove from the heat and sprinkle evenly over the bottom:

1 cup sugar

Arrange a ring of apple quarters against the sides of the pan, standing the apples on the thin edge of their cut side so as to fit as many as possible. Fill in the center of the skillet with the remaining apple quarters. You may have a piece or two of apple left over.

Place the skillet over the highest possible heat and cook until the juices turn from butterscotch to deep amber, 10 to 12 minutes. Remove the skillet from the heat,

spear the apples with a fork or the point of a paring knife, and flip them onto their uncooked sides. Return the skillet to high heat and boil 5 minutes more. Remove the skillet from the heat and slide the prepared crust onto the apples. Being careful not to burn your fingers, gently tuck the edges of the dough against the inner sides of the skillet.

Bake the tart until the crust is richly browned, 25 to 35 minutes. Let cool on a rack for 20 minutes, then loosen the sides with a knife and invert the tart onto a serving plate that can withstand heat. Return any apples that stick to the skillet to their proper place on top of the tart. Serve immediately or let stand at room temperature for up to 8 hours. When ready to serve, warm the tart to tepid in an oven heated at the lowest setting. Accompany with:

Sour Cream Whipped Topping, below, crème fraîche, or vanilla ice cream

Sour Cream Whipped Topping

About 2⅔ cups; 8 to 12 servings

A tangy topping that is lovely with a warm apple or pear tart.

Combine in a medium bowl:

1 cup cold heavy cream

½ cup cold sour cream

Beat on high speed until soft but definite peaks form. Do not attempt to whip until stiff. Use at once, or cover and refrigerate for up to 1 day.

Open-Faced Peach Custard Pie

One 9-inch pie; 8 servings

A JOY classic.

Prepare in a 9-inch pie pan, glazing with the egg yolk:

Baked Flaky Pastry Crust, 22

Position a rack in the lower third of the oven. Preheat the oven to 400°F. Whisk together until well blended:

1 large egg or 2 large egg yolks

¾ cup sugar

6 tablespoons (¾ stick) unsalted butter, melted

⅓ cup all-purpose flour

1 teaspoon vanilla

¼ teaspoon salt

Arrange in a single layer, cut side down, over the bottom of the crust:

3 to 4 fresh peaches, peeled and halved, or 6 to 8 drained canned peach halves

Pour the egg mixture over the peaches. Bake the pie for 10 minutes. Reduce the oven temperature to 300°F and bake until the custard is brown and crusty on top and appears firmly set in the center when the pan is shaken, about 1 hour longer. Let cool on a rack. Serve warm or at room temperature. The pie can be stored refrigerated for up to 1 day. If you wish, accompany with:

Whipped Cream, 76

PEELING PEACHES

To peel a peach, dip the fruit in boiling water for 20 to 60 seconds, depending on the size and density of the fruit, lift out and drop in cold water to cool, then slip off the skin. Because peach flesh darkens when exposed to air, peel a peach at the last minute or, to prevent browning: Sprinkle any citrus juice over the fruit and gently toss to coat all surfaces; or drop the fruit in a bowl of water acidulated with lemon juice.

Linzertorte

One 9½-inch torte; 8 to 10 servings

Named after the Austrian town of Linz, the traditional linzertorte is a lattice-top tart made with a rich and crumbly nut crust and filled with raspberry or currant jam. Other jams, preserves, and marmalades can be substituted, as can fruit butters. Linzertorte actually improves in flavor for 2 to 3 days after baking and keeps for at least 1 week.

Position a rack in the center of the oven. Preheat the oven to 350°F. Spread on a baking sheet:

¾ cup slivered blanched almonds or whole hazelnuts

Toast in the oven, stirring occasionally, until golden, 5 to 7 minutes. If using hazelnuts with skins, rub the nuts a handful a time in a thick towel to remove as much of the skins as possible. Turn off the oven. Let the nuts cool completely, then finely grind in a blender or food processor. Remove to a large bowl and whisk in thoroughly:

1⅓ cups all-purpose flour
½ cup powdered sugar
1 tablespoon unsweetened cocoa (optional)

1 teaspoon ground cinnamon
¼ teaspoon ground cloves
¼ teaspoon salt
Add:
10 tablespoons (1¼ sticks) unsalted butter, softened
2 large egg yolks
Grated zest of 1 medium lemon

Mix on low speed with an electric mixer or cream with the back of a wooden spoon until a smooth dough forms. Press the dough into a thick, flat disk, wrap in plastic, and refrigerate for at least 2 hours or up to 2 days.

Position a rack in the center of the oven. Preheat the oven to 350°F. Have ready a two-piece 9½- or 10-inch tart pan.

Let the dough warm at room temperature until malleable but firm, 30 minutes to 1 hour. Set aside one-quarter of the dough for the lattice. With your hands, press the remaining dough evenly over the bottom and sides of the tart pan. Roll the remaining dough into a 10-inch square between 2 sheets of plastic wrap or

wax paper. Remove the top sheet of plastic or paper and cut the dough into 8 to 12 strips of equal width. If the strips are too soft to handle, refrigerate or freeze them until firm. Spread evenly over the crust:

1½ cups raspberry jam

The layer should be about ¼ inch thick. Carefully arrange half of the dough strips on the tart at equal distance from each other; pinch the ends onto the crust. Arrange the remaining strips on top at right angles to those beneath, forming a crisscross lattice. If the strips break during handling, simply piece them together; they will fuse during baking. Bake until the lattice is golden brown, 40 to 45 minutes. Let cool completely on a rack. Remove the side of the pan, leaving the bottom in place beneath the torte. Wrap airtight and store in the refrigerator for up to 1 week or freeze for up to 1 month. Let warm to room temperature before serving *mit Schlag*, that is, with:

Whipped Cream, 76

Galettes

A galette—or in Italian, a *crostata*—consists of a flat crust of pastry or bread dough covered with sugar, pastry cream, or a thin layer of fruit. The famed French *Galette des Rois*, or Twelfth Night cake, is made with puff pastry. Sometimes it is baked with an elaborately decorated top crust and filled with a rich almond cream. Most galettes, however, are more simply made and rustic in look. They are, in effect, dessert pizzas.

Since galettes are baked on a flat baking sheet rather than in a pie or tart mold, they may be made in any shape, such as a square, rectangle, or circle, that appeals to you. If the filling is juicy, bring the edge of the crust over the filling to catch drips; otherwise, simply double up the crust edge, then crimp or flute if you wish. The recipes that follow convey the basic technique. Use them to create your own variations, remembering that the galette or *crostata* topping should be spare so as not to overwhelm the crust.

Apple Galette

8 servings

This is a bit like a pizza, with thinly sliced apples on a buttery crust. Please read the note for Apple Pie I, 38, *for other suitable pie apples.*
Prepare:
½ recipe Deluxe Butter Flaky Pastry Dough, 17
Position a rack in the lower third of

the oven. Preheat the oven to 425°F. On a sheet of parchment paper or aluminum foil, roll the dough into an 11- to 12-inch round. Pick up the edges of the paper and transfer with the dough to a baking sheet. Melt and cool to lukewarm:
3 tablespoons unsalted butter

Brush a thin coat of butter over the pastry, reserving the rest. Sprinkle the pastry with:
1 tablespoon sugar
Peel, core, and slice ⅛ inch thick:
2 large firm apples, such as Golden Delicious
Leaving bare a 1-inch border at the edge, arrange the apple slices in slightly overlapping concentric rings on the pastry. Fold the border of dough over the edge of the apples. Brush or drizzle all but about 2 teaspoons of the remaining melted butter over the apples. Combine, then sprinkle over the apples:
3 tablespoons sugar
⅛ teaspoon ground cinnamon
Bake until the pastry begins to color, 15 to 20 minutes. Reduce the oven temperature to 350°F and bake until the pastry is golden brown and sounds crisp when poked with a skewer, 20 to 30 minutes more. Set the pan on a rack, brush the apples with the remaining butter, and let cool. Serve warm or at room temperature. The galette is best served the day it is made.

Fruit Crostata

8 servings

In Italy, cherished recipes for this favorite rustic tart are handed down from generation to generation. This recipe calls for a pat-in-the-pan shortbread crust instead of the typical flaky pastry crust. Use ripe fruit picked at the peak of the season.

Prepare the dough for:

Shortbread Crust, 28

Refrigerate the dough until firm but malleable, like modeling clay. Position a rack in the lower third of the oven. Preheat the oven to 375°F.

Lightly flour the dough, then roll it into an 11-inch round between 2 sheets of parchment paper (available at kitchen supply stores). Peel off the top sheet of paper. Lift the dough on the bottom sheet of paper onto a large baking sheet. Leaving bare a 1-inch border at the edge, spread evenly over the crust:

¼ cup raspberry or other jam

Fold over the border to form a rim. Toss together gently:

4 medium plums or 2 peeled medium peaches, pitted and cut into ½-inch pieces
½ cup raspberries or blueberries (optional)
2 tablespoons sugar
1 tablespoon plus 1 teaspoon all-purpose flour

Distribute the fruit mixture over the jam. Bake the *crostata* until the crust is golden brown and the fruit juices have thickened, 25 to 35 minutes. Let cool slightly before serving.

Yeasted French Galette

8 servings

Each region of France has its own special version of this rich, yeasted galette, which turns out to be surprisingly similar to the Moravian sugar cake of Pennsylvania Dutch baking. Yeasty, buttery, light, and airy, this French galette (opposite, front) is a cross between cake and bread. Serve the galette as an informal dessert, or at breakfast or brunch, or with tea or coffee.

Stir together in a small bowl and let stand 10 minutes:

⅓ cup lukewarm water
1 envelope active dry yeast

In a medium bowl, cream with the back of a spoon until smooth:

12 tablespoons (1½ sticks)
unsalted butter, softened
⅓ cup sugar
1 large egg
Grated zest of 2 lemons

Stir in the yeast mixture, then beat in:

1¾ cups all-purpose flour
⅛ teaspoon salt

Cover the bowl tightly with plastic wrap and let the dough stand in a warm place for 3 hours. It will become slightly spongy but it will not rise.

Position a rack in the center of the oven. Preheat the oven to 450°F. Butter a large baking sheet, sprinkle with sugar, and tilt in all directions until evenly coated. Scrape the dough onto the prepared baking sheet and sprinkle lightly with sugar. Cover with plastic wrap and press into an 11-inch round. Carefully remove the plastic wrap. Fold over the edge ¾ inch to form a rim all around. Dot the top of the galette with:

3 tablespoons cold unsalted butter, cut into ¼-inch bits

Sprinkle with:

2 tablespoons sugar

Refrigerate the galette for 10 minutes, then bake until golden brown, 8 to 10 minutes. Let cool on a wire rack. Serve warm or at room temperature. The galette is best served the day it is made.

Half-Covered Berry or Peach Galette

8 servings

In making this galette (opposite, back), you roll the crust extra wide and then fold the edges over the fruit, leaving the fruit exposed in the center. A cornmeal crust works well here.

Prepare:

½ recipe Cornmeal Flaky Pastry Dough, 17, or ½ recipe Deluxe Butter Flaky Pastry Dough, 17

Position a rack in the lower third of the oven. Preheat the oven to 400°F. On a well-floured work surface, roll the dough into a 13-inch round. Carefully slide a rimless cookie sheet beneath the dough, letting the edges of the dough overhang the sides of the sheet. Leaving bare a 2- to 3-inch border, arrange in the center of the dough:

1½ cups blueberries and/or raspberries, or thinly sliced peeled peaches

Scatter evenly over the fruit:

2 tablespoons sugar
1 tablespoon cold unsalted butter, cut into small pieces

Fold the border of dough over the fruit, forming a pleated half cover, with the fruit exposed in the center. Light brush the dough with:

Milk

Sprinkle with:

1 to 2 teaspoons sugar

Bake the galette until golden brown, 25 to 35 minutes. Let cool on a rack. Serve warm or at room temperature. The galette is best served the day it is made.

BLUEBERRIES

Blueberries are sweet with enough tang to make them interesting. Blue on the outside and light green on the inside, cultivated blueberries are much larger than their wild forebears. Choose plump, sound berries nicely covered with bloom, a whitish coating that preserves the moisture in blueberries and helps them keep longer than most other berries. As delicious as blueberries are raw, they are the perfect baking berry—from pies and pancakes to muffins and cheesecake topping. Blueberries both freeze and dry superbly and are good canned as well.

ABOUT **CREAM** PIES

Cream pies are simply prebaked crusts filled with easy-to-make stovetop cornstarch puddings. Once chilled, they are topped with whimsical swirls of fluffy meringue or whipped cream.

Chiffon, mousse, and ice cream pies all have featherweight fillings that are poured into prebaked crusts and then chilled, just like cream pies. Chiffon pie is made of a custard sauce stiffened with gelatin and lightened with whipped egg whites. Mousse pies have airy, melt-on-the-tongue fillings. Ice cream pies are the ultimate no-fuss dessert. Quick to assemble, they are guaranteed to bring smiles to the table.

All of these pies are perfect for entertaining since they need time in the refrigerator (or freezer, for ice cream pies) for their fillings to set. Make them in advance and then spend time with your guests instead of in the kitchen.

Vanilla Cream Pie, 74

Fillings for Cream Pies

Cream pie filling is simply a cornstarch pudding made on top of the stove and enriched with egg yolks. In order to avoid scorching, stir the filling constantly as it cooks with a wooden spoon or heatproof rubber spatula, reaching all corners of the saucepan. To prevent lumps, remove the filling from the heat as it approaches the simmer and begins to thicken, and whisk vigorously. After whisking, return the filling to the heat, bring it to a full simmer, and cook for 30 seconds. If this is not done, amylase, an enzyme in the egg yolks, will react with the starch, thinning out and discoloring the filling within 24 hours. The filling is also likely to thin out if allowed to cool before being poured into the crust, so spoon the filling into the crust immediately after cooking. Contrary to popular belief, hot filling does not cause the crust to become soggy. The cream pies in this section can be made up to 1 day ahead and refrigerated.

Vanilla Cream Pie

One 9-inch pie; 8 servings

This not only is a scrumptious pie on its own but also provides the base for three classic variations, right.
If topping the pie with meringue, position a rack in the center of the oven and preheat the oven to 325°F.
Prepare in a 9-inch pie pan:
Baked Flaky Pastry Crust, 22, a pat-in-the-pan crust, 26 to 29, or Crumb Crust, 30
Whisk in a medium, heavy saucepan until well blended:
⅔ cup sugar
¼ cup cornstarch
¼ teaspoon salt
Gradually whisk in:
2½ cups whole milk
Vigorously whisk in until the egg yolks are completely blended and no yellow streaks remain:
5 large egg yolks
Stirring constantly with a wooden spoon or heatproof rubber spatula, bring the mixture to a bare simmer over medium heat. Remove from the heat, scrape the corners of the saucepan with the spoon or spatula, and whisk until smooth. Return to the heat and, whisking constantly, bring to a simmer and cook for 30 seconds. Remove the pan from the heat and whisk in:
2 to 3 tablespoons unsalted butter, cut into small pieces
1 tablespoon vanilla
Spoon the filling into the prepared crust and press a sheet of plastic wrap directly on the surface. If you are covering the pie with meringue, proceed at once to prepare:
Soft Meringue Topping, 31
Remove the plastic wrap and spread the meringue over the top of the pie, anchoring it to the crust rim on all sides. Bake the pie for 20 minutes, let cool completely on a rack, and then refrigerate. If not using a meringue, simply refrigerate the pie for at least 3 hours to firm the filling. Shortly before serving, remove the plastic wrap and cover the pie with:
Whipped Cream, 76

BANANA CREAM PIE

To keep the bananas from browning, slice them just before filling the pie.
Prepare the crust and filling for *Vanilla Cream Pie, left.* Thinly slice 2 to 4 firm ripe bananas, enough to measure 1½ to 2 cups. Spoon a third of the filling into the pie shell and scatter half of the bananas over the top. Cover with another third of the filling and then the rest of the bananas. Spread the remaining filling over the top (opposite, back).

CHOCOLATE CREAM PIE

We can never decide if we prefer this old-fashioned pie with a whipped cream or a meringue topping. Whipped cream has the edge for those who like to decorate the top with grated semisweet chocolate.
Prepare *Vanilla Cream Pie, left,* but increase the sugar to 1 cup and decrease the cornstarch to 3 tablespoons. Finely chop 4 ounces unsweetened baking chocolate, add it with the butter, and stir until the chocolate melts.

COCONUT CREAM PIE

Wonderful served with Caramel Sauce Cockaigne, 83, *or a chocolate sauce.*
Spread 1 to 1⅓ cups shredded sweetened dried coconut in a 9-inch cake pan and toast, stirring occasionally, in a 300°F oven until golden brown, 20 to 30 minutes. Prepare *Vanilla Cream Pie, left,* adding the coconut to the filling along with the butter (opposite, front).

Black Bottom Pie

One 10-inch pie; 8 to 10 servings

A JOY classic first appearing in the 1946 edition, this two-toned, whipped cream–topped, chocolate and vanilla-rum cream pie continues to please today. Before beginning, please read Egg Safety, 79.

Prepare and bake in a 10-inch pie pan:

Crumb Crust, 30, preferably made with gingersnaps

Pour into a small cup:

¼ cup cold water

Sprinkle over the top and let stand for 5 minutes:

1½ teaspoons (¾ envelope) unfla-vored gelatin

Place in a small bowl:

6 ounces bittersweet or semisweet chocolate, finely chopped, or 1 cup semisweet chocolate chips

Whisk together thoroughly in a medium, heavy saucepan:

⅓ cup sugar

4 teaspoons cornstarch

Gradually whisk in:

2 cups light cream, or 1 cup milk and 1 cup heavy cream

Vigorously whisk in until no yellow streaks remain:

4 large egg yolks

Stirring constantly with a wooden spoon or heatproof rubber spatula, bring the mixture to a simmer over medium heat and cook for 30 seconds. Remove from the heat. Immediately stir 1 cup of the mixture into the chocolate. Add the softened gelatin to the remaining mixture in the pan and stir for 30 seconds to dissolve the gelatin. Vigorously stir the chocolate mixture until smooth; if the chocolate fails to melt completely, set the bottom of the bowl in very hot water. Spread the chocolate mixture evenly over the bottom of the pie crust and refrigerate. Stir into

the custard in the pan:

2 tablespoons dark rum

2 teaspoons vanilla

Beat on medium speed until foamy:

3 large egg whites

Add:

¼ teaspoon cream of tartar

Continue to beat until soft peaks form, then gradually beat in:

⅓ cup plus 1 tablespoon sugar

Increase the speed to high and beat until the peaks are stiff and glossy. Using a large rubber spatula, gently fold the egg whites into the custard mixture. Spoon the filling over the chocolate mixture. Refrigerate for at least 3 hours or up to 1 day. Shortly before serving, spread over the top of the pie:

Whipped Cream, below

If you wish, sprinkle with:

1 ounce bittersweet or semisweet chocolate, grated or shaved

Whipped Cream

2 to 2½ cups

In a chilled bowl with chilled beaters, beat until thickened:

1 cup cold heavy cream

If you wish, add and beat to the desired consistency:

2 teaspoons to 2 tablespoons sugar, 1 to 4 tablespoons sifted powdered sugar, or 2 teaspoons honey (optional)

½ teaspoon vanilla (optional)

Use immediately or cover and refrigerate up to several hours.

Lemon or Lime Chiffon Pie

One 9-inch pie; 6 to 8 servings

A chiffon pie is one whose filling is based on a custard sauce stiffened with gelatin. The secret is a deft, gentle hand in folding the aerated egg whites into the gelatin filling. Tart and sprightly, this has long been America's favorite chiffon pie. Before beginning, please read Egg Safety, opposite.

Prepare in a 9-inch pie pan:

Baked Flaky Pastry Crust, 22, *a pat-in-the-pan crust*, 26 to 29, or Crumb Crust, 30

Pour into a small, heavy saucepan:

¼ cup water

Sprinkle over the top and let stand for 5 minutes:

1 envelope (2¼ teaspoons) unflavored gelatin

Whisk in:

½ cup water

½ cup strained fresh lemon or lime juice

1 teaspoon grated lemon or lime zest

⅓ cup plus 1 tablespoon sugar

4 large egg yolks

Stirring constantly with a wooden spoon or heatproof rubber spatula, heat over medium heat until the mixture begins to steam and coats the spoon or spatula fairly heavily. Do not allow to simmer, or it will become grainy. Immediately pour the mixture into a large bowl and refrigerate for 45 minutes to 1 hour, or until it forms little mounds when dropped from a spoon. Be careful not to let the gelatin set too firmly. Beat in a clean mixer bowl on medium speed until foamy:

4 large egg whites

Add:

¼ teaspoon cream of tartar

Continue to beat until the egg whites form soft peaks (**1**), then gradually beat in:

½ cup sugar

Increase the speed to high and beat until the peaks are stiff and glossy (**2**). Using a large rubber spatula, gently fold the egg whites into the gelatin mixture (**3**). Spoon the filling into the crust, mounding it in the center, and refrigerate for at least 4 hours or up to 1 day.

SOAKING AND DISSOLVING GELATIN

Gelatin dishes will develop a grainy, rubbery skin and may refuse to set unless the gelatin is handled in two distinct steps. First, soak the gelatin in a small amount of *cold* liquid for at least 5 minutes to allow the granules to soften and swell; then dissolve the gelatin completely in *hot* liquid. If the mixture is transparent, you can tell if the gelatin has dissolved simply by dipping in a metal spoon and allowing the liquid to run off: The glaze on the spoon will be completely clear, without any sign of beading. In the case of an opaque mixture, stir until the spoon or spatula seems to slip and slide over the bottom of the bowl or pot. As long as the gelatin is fully softened and your liquid is steaming hot, the gelatin is virtually guaranteed to melt after 30 seconds of gentle stirring.

Chocolate Mousse Pie

One 10-inch pie; 10 servings

In contrast to chiffon pies, if the filling is not stiffened with gelatin, call it a mousse. Mousse pies soften quickly at room temperature and become impossible to slice neatly, so leave them in the refrigerator until just before serving. This pie has become an American favorite. A plain chocolate mousse makes a soft, lush filling; a chocolate mousse with gelatin yields a slightly stiffer filling that holds its shape well. This dessert is made with uncooked eggs; see Egg Safety, below.

Prepare and bake in a 10-inch pie pan:

Crumb Crust, 30, made with chocolate wafers

Let the crust cool completely. Heat 1 inch water in a large skillet over low heat until bubbles form along the bottom; adjust the heat to maintain the water at this temperature. Combine in a large heatproof bowl:

6 ounces semisweet or bittersweet chocolate, chopped

3 tablespoons unsalted butter

2 tablespoons liquor, liqueur, coffee, or water

1 teaspoon vanilla if using water

Set the bowl in the water bath and stir until the chocolate is melted. Remove from the water and set aside. Whisk together thoroughly in a heatproof bowl:

3 large egg yolks

3 tablespoons coffee or water

3 tablespoons sugar

Set the bowl in the water bath and, whisking constantly, heat the mixture until thick and puffy, like marshmallow sauce, and warm to the touch. Remove from the water bath and whisk thoroughly into the melted chocolate. Let cool to room temperature. In a separate bowl, beat on medium speed until foamy:

3 large egg whites, at room temperature

Add and beat until soft peaks form:

¼ teaspoon cream of tartar

Gradually beat in:

¼ cup sugar

Increase the speed to high and beat until the peaks are stiff. Using a large rubber spatula, stir one-quarter of the egg whites into the chocolate mixture to lighten it, then gently fold in the remaining whites. In another bowl, beat on medium-high speed until soft peaks form:

½ cup cold heavy cream

Gently but thoroughly fold the cream into the chocolate mixture. Spread the filling in the pie shell. Refrigerate the pie for at least 3 hours to set the filling. Shortly before serving, beat on medium speed until thickened:

1 cup cold heavy cream

Add:

¼ cup powdered sugar

½ teaspoon vanilla

Whip until stiff peaks form. Spread the whipped cream over the top of the pie. If you wish, sprinkle with:

1 ounce bittersweet or semisweet chocolate, grated or shaved

Store refrigerated for up to 1 day.

EGG SAFETY

The bacteria *Salmonella enteritidis*, which can cause illness and even death, is occasionally found in raw eggs, even uncracked eggs. While the risk remains extremely low (it is estimated that 1 in 10,000 eggs is infected, and even infected eggs may not cause problems if properly stored and cooked), we recommend handling eggs carefully, particularly when cooking for young children, the elderly, pregnant women, or anyone with a compromised immune system. Buy refrigerated eggs and get them to your own refrigerator as quickly as possible. Never use a doubtful egg. When cracking or separating eggs, make sure that the fresh egg never touches the exterior of the shell, which is more apt to carry contamination. Before and after handling eggs, wash your hands and any utensils or equipment that may have come into contact with either the shell or the contents.

CHOCOLATE MOUSSE PIE WITH GELATIN

Gelatin firms up the filling and makes for neater slices.

Sprinkle 1½ teaspoons (⅔ envelope) unflavored gelatin over 3 tablespoons cold coffee or water and let soak for at least 5 minutes. Prepare *Chocolate Mousse Pie, above*, substituting the gelatin mixture for the 3 tablespoons plain coffee or water added to the egg yolks.

Chocolate Almond Candy Bar Pie

One 10-inch pie; 10 servings

A gooey chocolate mousse in a thick, crunchy crust made from cream-filled chocolate sandwich cookies.

Position a rack in the center of the oven. Preheat the oven to 400°F. Lightly butter a 10-inch pie pan. Place in a sturdy plastic bag:

**30 cream-filled chocolate sand-
   wich cookies**

Crush with a rolling pin to coarse ¼-inch pieces. Transfer to a mixing bowl and combine well with:

**6 tablespoons (¾ stick) unsalted
   butter, melted**

Pat the mixture over the bottom and sides of the pie pan. Bake for 7 minutes, then let cool completely on a rack. Tear or snip into quarters:

24 large marshmallows

Chop into ¼-inch pieces:

**1 pound milk chocolate candy bars
   with almonds**

Stirring with a wooden spoon or heatproof rubber spatula, bring to a boil in a large saucepan over medium heat:

1 cup heavy cream

Set aside 3 tablespoons of the chopped chocolate bars for decorating. Add the remaining to the boiling cream and stir until the chocolate melts. Remove the pan from the heat, stir in the marshmallows, tightly cover, and let stand for 5 minutes. Very gently fold the softened marshmallows into the chocolate mixture, retaining as much air in the mixture as possible. (There may be a few unblended bits of marshmallow.) Pour the filling into the crust and refrigerate for 4 hours. If not serving the pie at once, press a sheet of plastic wrap directly onto the surface and refrigerate for up to 2 days. Shortly before serving, beat on medium speed until thickened:

1 cup cold heavy cream

Add:

¼ cup powdered sugar
½ teaspoon vanilla

Whip until stiff peaks form. Spread the whipped cream over the top of the pie. Sprinkle with the reserved chopped chocolate bars (opposite).

Peanut Butter Pie

One 10-inch pie; 8 to 10 servings

This may sound like kids' stuff, but it's not. The filling is mousselike and surprisingly subtle in flavor, and the chocolate glaze gives the pie a finished, elegant look.

Prepare and bake in a 10-inch pie pan:

**Crumb Crust, 30, made with graham
   crackers or chocolate wafers**

Beat on medium speed just until smoothly blended:

8 ounces cream cheese, softened
**1 cup chunky or smooth peanut
   butter**
½ cup sugar
2 teaspoons vanilla

In a separate bowl, beat on medium-high speed until stiff peaks form:

1 cup cold heavy cream

Using a large rubber spatula, fold half of the whipped cream into the peanut butter mixture to lighten it, then fold in the remaining cream.

Spread the mixture evenly in the pie crust. Press a sheet of plastic wrap directly on the surface and refrigerate until firm, about 4 hours.

Stirring, bring to a boil in a medium saucepan over high heat:

⅓ cup heavy cream
2 tablespoons unsalted butter

Remove from the heat and immediately stir in until smooth:

**4 ounces bittersweet or semisweet
   chocolate, finely chopped**

Let cool to lukewarm, then pour the glaze over the top of the pie and spread evenly. If you wish, sprinkle with:

⅓ cup chopped salted peanuts

Refrigerate for at least 1 hour or up to 3 days. Accompany with:

Whipped Cream, 76

CREAM

Cream is made from the fat that rises to the surface of nonhomogenized milk. Sweet, or noncultured, creams are sold in pasteurized and ultrapasteurized forms.

Heavy cream contains at least 36 percent milk fat and is the richest cream available in most stores. It is often labled "whipping cream." It is normally used in desserts. Light cream contains 30 to 36 percent butterfat. Use heavy cream for whipping. It mounds easily and holds its shape well. It is used in all manner of dessert preparations.

Before beginning to whip the cream, first chill the cream, bowl, and whisk or beaters to facilitate the thickening process.

Ice Cream Pies

Pies filled with ice cream—or frozen yogurt, sherbet, or sorbet—are quick and simple to assemble, and you can create as many different varieties as there are flavors of ice cream in your grocer's freezer case. Start with a *Crumb Crust, 30,* or *Meringue Pie Crust, 31;* other crusts are flavorless and rock hard when frozen. Freeze the baked pie shell thoroughly before filling it, or the ice cream will melt along the bottom, soaking into the crust and fusing it to the pie pan. It is essential to use a premium brand of ice cream. Bargain brands are fluffed up with air and will deflate, losing as much as half their volume, when softened and packed into the shell. Let the ice cream or other frozen product soften to the point where it can easily be packed into the shell, but do not let it liquefy, or it will turn coarse and icy when it refreezes.

About 30 minutes before serving, allow the pie to soften slightly in the refrigerator. If, as often happens, the pie sticks to the pan when sliced, hold the bottom of the pan in a bowl of warm water for about 30 seconds.

Ice Cream Pie

One 10-inch pie; 8 to 10 servings

Use this basic recipe as a starting point and give your imagination free rein.
Bake in a 10-inch pie pan:

Crumb Crust, 30, or Meringue Pie Crust, 31

Let cool to room temperature, then freeze for at least 1 hour before filling. Meanwhile, let stand in the refrigerator until just soft enough to pack:

1½ to 2 quarts ice cream, frozen yogurt, sherbet, or sorbet

If you wish, have ready:

1 to 1½ cups crushed cream-filled chocolate sandwich cookies, chopped nougat-filled candy bars, or chocolate-covered peanut butter cups

Working quickly, pack half of the ice cream into the shell with the back of a large spoon. If you are using them, sprinkle half of the crushed cookies or chopped candies over the top and press in firmly. Pack the remaining ice cream in the shell, mounding it in the center, then sprinkle with the rest of the cookies or candies and again press them in. Smooth a sheet of plastic wrap on the surface of the pie and freeze until solid, at least 2 hours or up to 2 days. About 30 minutes before serving, transfer the pie to the refrigerator to allow it to soften slightly. If you wish, use a pastry bag fitted with a large star tip to pipe over the top of the pie:

Whipped Cream, 76

Decorate with:

Crushed cookies, chopped candies, or toasted nuts (optional)

Serve the pie with:

A chocolate sauce, a caramel sauce such as *Caramel Sauce Cockaigne* (opposite), a fresh fruit sauce, or a cooked fruit sauce

Caramel Sauce Cockaigne

About 1 ½ cups; 8 to 10 servings

One of the most luxurious versions of caramel sauce.

Place in a small, heavy saucepan:

1 cup sugar

Pour evenly over the top:

¼ cup water

Place the pan over medium-high heat and, without stirring, swirl the saucepan gently by the handle until the sugar is dissolved and the syrup is clear. Avoid letting the syrup boil until the sugar is completely dissolved. Increase the heat to high, cover the saucepan tightly, and boil the syrup for 2 minutes. Uncover the saucepan and continue to boil the syrup until it begins to darken around the edges. Gently swirl the pan by the handle until the syrup turns a deep amber and begins to smoke. Remove from the heat and add carefully (the mixture will splatter):

8 tablespoons (1 stick) unsalted butter, cut into pieces

Gently mix until the butter is incorporated. Stir in:

½ cup heavy cream

If the sauce becomes lumpy, set the pan over low heat and stir until smooth. Turn off the heat and stir in:

2 teaspoons vanilla

Pinch of salt

Serve warm or at room temperature. The sauce can be covered and refrigerated for up to 1 month; it will become solid. Reheat in a double boiler or in a heavy saucepan over very low heat, adding a bit of water if it is too thick.

ABOUT **CUSTARD** PIES

*C*ustard pies are what most people think of as quintessentially American. There is the traditional and deeply satisfying Custard Pie, 86—composed of eggs, sugar and milk perfumed with vanilla and nutmeg. Then there are the Pumpkin and Sweet Potato Pies, 88 to 91, *without which holiday tables at Thanksgiving would be woefully incomplete.* Pecan, Chess, *and even the distantly-related, not-so-custardy* Shoofly Pies, 93 to 95—*longtime Southern favorites—round out the custard pie family.*

Custard pies are treasured for their sweet, creamy, smooth filling. The trick to baking a custard pie with a perfect consistency—without the slightest trace of graininess—is actually quite simple: Make sure the prebaked pie crust is warm before pouring in the filling. If the crust is cool, slip it into a warm oven for several minutes and then proceed.

Coconut Custard Pie, 86

Custard Pie

Like all custards, fillings for custard pies need to be baked at a relatively low temperature to keep from curdling, but the crust tends to become soggy unless the pie is baked at a high heat. In our 1975 edition we suggested baking the custard and crust separately in 2 pie pans of identical size and then slipping the filling into the shell just before serving. This sleight-of-hand works surprisingly well, but we have since discovered that it is possible to make custard pie in a more conventional way and still get excellent results. The trick is to have both the custard and the crust hot when the pie is assembled. This allows the custard to set quickly at the comfortably low temperature it favors, and thus the crust does not become soaked. For this trick to work, you must use a flaky pastry crust, fully baked and carefully moisture-proofed with egg yolk; pat-in-the-pan crusts inevitably become sodden. To prevent the filling from overcooking and turning grainy around the edges, custard pie must be removed from the oven when the center is still quivery, like gelatin. The filling will continue to cook on stored heat as the pie stands and will thicken further upon cooling. Because custard pie is highly susceptible to spoilage, refrigerate it as soon as it has cooled to room temperature. Serve the pie within a day of baking, or the crust will soften.

Custard Pie

One 9-inch pie; 6 to 8 servings

A thoroughly satisfying pie that has changed little since its first appearance in American cookbooks nearly two centuries ago.

Position a rack in the center of the oven. Preheat the oven to 325°F. Prepare in a 9-inch pie pan, preferably glass, glazing with the egg yolk:

Baked Flaky Pastry Crust, 22

If the crust has cooled, warm it in the oven for up to 10 minutes while you prepare the filling. Whisk together just until blended:

3 large eggs
2 to 3 large egg yolks
½ cup sugar
1 teaspoon vanilla
⅛ teaspoon salt

Stirring, bring to a simmer in a small saucepan over medium heat:

2 cups whole milk

Gently whisking all the while, gradually add the milk to the egg mixture. Immediately pour the hot custard into the warmed crust. Dust the top with:

½ to 1 teaspoon freshly grated or ground nutmeg

Bake until the center of the custard seems set but quivery, like gelatin, when the pan is nudged, 25 to 35 minutes. Let cool completely on a rack, then refrigerate for up to 1 day. Let warm to room temperature for 1 hour before serving.

CHOCOLATE-FROSTED CUSTARD PIE

A great favorite in our grandmother's day and overdue for a revival.
Prepare *Custard Pie, left,* omitting the nutmeg; let cool to room temperature. Finely chop 3 ounces bittersweet or semisweet chocolate. Bring ⅓ cup heavy cream and 2 tablespoons sugar to a boil in a small saucepan, stirring to dissolve the sugar. Remove from the heat, add the chocolate, and stir until melted. Let cool slightly, then spread over the top of the pie. Refrigerate until the glaze sets.

COCONUT CUSTARD PIE

This classic pie has a delicious, subtle coconut flavor.
Prepare *Custard Pie, left,* sprinkling the crust with 1 to 1¼ cups shredded sweetened dried coconut or finely shredded fresh coconut before pouring in the custard.

NUTMEG

Nutmeg comes from the brown, oval seed of a fruit resembling an apricot, which grows on a tropical evergreen tree. Wrapped around the shell of the seed is a lacy sheath—the spice mace—which is ground before packing. Several weeks after harvest, when the kernel has shrunk in the seed shell, the thin shell is cracked and the kernel removed. This is nutmeg—brown, solid, and hard. Nutmeg is a warm spice best when freshly grated.

Pumpkin, Sweet Potato, and Squash Pies

Although these pies are made with cooked vegetable purees, structurally speaking they are actually custard pies and should be handled in a similar way. To set the filling quickly and thus prevent a soggy crust, have the filling at room temperature and the crust warm. If the pie is overbaked, the filling will be coarse and watery around the edges, so remove the pie from the oven as soon as the center quivers like gelatin when the pan is nudged. The pie will continue to set up as it cools. Eat the pie within a day of baking, or the crust will soften.

Fresh Pumpkin: Jack-o'-lantern pumpkins make poor pies; look for an eating variety, such as Small Sugar, at a specialty market. You will need 5 to 6 pounds pumpkin to make 4 cups of puree, or enough for 2 pies. Split the pumpkins into quarters, cut out the stem, scrape out the pulp, and hack into 4-inch pieces. Place rind side down in an oiled roasting pan, cover tightly with aluminum foil, and bake at 325°F until very soft, about 1½ hours. Scrape out the flesh and puree in a food processor. If the puree seems loose and wet, drain in cheesecloth for 30 to 60 minutes, or until it reaches the same consistency as the canned kind.

Fresh Winter Squash: Prepare fresh squash as for pumpkin, using a firm, dense, sweet variety such as butternut or Hubbard. Squash is quite moist and requires thorough draining in cheesecloth as directed for pumpkin.

Pumpkin Pie

One 9-inch pie; 8 servings

Use 3 eggs for a soft, custardy filling, 2 for a firmer pie.

Position a rack in the center of the oven. Preheat the oven to 375°F. Building up a high fluted rim, prepare in a 9-inch pie pan, preferably glass, glazing with the egg yolk:

Baked Flaky Pastry Crust, 22, or Pat-in-the-Pan Butter Crust, 26

Whisk thoroughly in a large bowl:

2 to 3 large eggs (see note)

Whisk in thoroughly:

2 cups freshly cooked or canned pumpkin puree

1½ cups light cream or evaporated milk, or ¾ cup milk and ¾ cup heavy cream

½ cup sugar

⅓ cup firmly packed light or dark brown sugar

1 teaspoon ground cinnamon

1 teaspoon ground ginger

½ teaspoon freshly grated or ground nutmeg

¼ teaspoon ground cloves or allspice

½ teaspoon salt

Warm the pie crust in the oven until it is hot to the touch, letting the filling stand at room temperature in the meantime. Pour the pumpkin mixture into the crust and bake until the center of the filling seems set but quivery, like gelatin, when the pan is nudged, 35 to 45 minutes. Let cool completely on a rack, then refrigerate for up to 1 day. Serve cold, at room temperature, or slightly warmed. Accompany with:

Whipped Cream, 76, and/or Hot Brandy Sauce, below

Hot Brandy Sauce

Melt over low heat in a small, heavy saucepan:

8 tablespoons unsalted butter

Stir in, using a wooden spoon:

1 cup sugar

¼ cup brandy or Cognac

2 tablespoons water

¼ teaspoon freshly grated or ground nutmeg

⅛ teaspoon salt

Cook, stirring, until the sugar is dissolved and the mixture is blended. Remove from the heat. Whisk until light and frothy:

1 large egg

Vigorously whisk the egg into the liquor mixture. Set the sauce over medium heat and, stirring gently, bring to a simmer. Cook until thickened, about 1 minute. The sauce will not curdle. Serve at once, set aside at room temperature for up to 8 hours, or let cool, then cover and refrigerate for up to 3 days. Reheat over low heat, stirring; if the sauce separates, remove from the heat and whisk in a little warm water.

Sour Cream Pumpkin Pie

One 9-inch pie; 8 servings

A tangy pie with a light, soufflélike texture (opposite, front).

Position a rack in the center of the oven. Preheat the oven to 350°F. Building up a high fluted rim, prepare in a 9-inch pan, preferably glass, glazing with the egg yolk:

Baked Flaky Pastry Crust, 22, or Pat-in-the-Pan Butter Crust, 26

In a large, heavy saucepan, whisk together thoroughly:

1½ cups freshly cooked or canned pumpkin puree
8 ounces (scant 1 cup) sour cream
¾ cup sugar
3 large egg yolks
1 teaspoon ground cinnamon
½ teaspoon ground ginger
½ teaspoon freshly grated or ground nutmeg
¼ teaspoon ground cloves or allspice
¼ teaspoon salt

Whisking constantly, heat over medium heat until just warm to the touch. Beat on medium speed until foamy:

3 large egg whites, at room temperature

Add:

¼ teaspoon cream of tartar

Continue to beat until soft peaks form, then gradually beat in:

¼ cup sugar

Increase the speed to high and beat until the peaks are stiff and glossy. Using a large rubber spatula, gently fold the egg whites into the pumpkin mixture. Pour the filling into the prepared crust. Bake until the top has browned lightly and feels softly set when touched, 40 to 50 minutes. Let cool completely on a rack. At this point the pie can be refrigerated for up to 1 day. Let warm at room temperature for 30 minutes before serving. Serve with:

Whipped Cream, 76

Sweet Potato Pie

One 9-inch pie; 8 servings

A moist and creamy version of this Southern favorite (opposite, back).

Position a rack in the center of the oven. Preheat the oven to 400°F. Building up a high fluted rim, prepare in a 9-inch pie pan, preferably glass, glazing with the egg yolk:

Baked Flaky Pastry Crust, 22, or Pat-in-the-Pan Butter Crust, 26

Peel deeply, removing both skin and the pale, fibrous layer beneath it:

2 pounds sweet potatoes

Cut crosswise into 1-inch chunks and steam in a basket over boiling water until very tender, about 20 minutes. Puree in a food processor or force through a fine-mesh sieve with the back of a spoon. Measure 1⅓ cups puree. Whisk together thoroughly in a medium bowl:

4 large eggs
½ cup sugar

Whisk in the sweet potato puree, then whisk in:

1 cup light cream or evaporated milk, or ½ cup milk and ½ cup heavy cream
4 tablespoons (½ stick) unsalted butter, melted
4 teaspoons strained fresh lemon juice
1½ teaspoons vanilla
¾ teaspoon ground cinnamon
¾ teaspoon freshly grated or ground nutmeg
½ teaspoon salt

Warm the pie crust in the oven until it is hot to the touch. Pour in the filling and bake for 20 minutes. Reduce the oven temperature to 325°F and bake until the center of the filling seems set but quivery, like gelatin, when the pan is nudged, about 20 minutes more. Let cool completely on a rack, then refrigerate for up to 1 day. Serve at room temperature or warmed. Accompany with:

Whipped Cream, 76

SWEET POTATO PUDDING

By baking a dish of custard in a larger pan of water—a water bath—the cook partially insulates the custard from the oven's heat and thereby protects it from overcooking. Double the recipe for Sweet Potato Pie, above, omitting the crust. Pour the filling into a buttered shallow 2- to 3-quart baking dish. Bake at 350°F in a larger baking pan filled halfway with hot water until firm in the center, 45 to 60 minutes. Serve with Hot Brandy Sauce, 88.

Pecan, Chess, and Shoofly Pies

The filling of pecan pie is actually a sort of custard composed of sugar, butter, and eggs, and like all custards, it will curdle and break if subjected to excessive heat. The trick is to pull the pie from the oven as soon as the filling has thickened to a gelatin-like consistency in the center. Although soft coming out of the oven, the filling will firm up nicely by the time the pie has cooled to room temperature.

Chess pies, now chiefly a Southern specialty, are essentially pecan pies without the nuts. There are countless varieties and much has been written about them but their origins remain unknown. All are rich and intensely sweet, approximating candy. Chess pies, like pecan pies, are highly heat sensitive, and the same precautions must be observed when baking them.

Shoofly pie, a famous dessert of Pennsylvania Dutch country, is a distant relative of the pecan and chess family. Because the filling is thickened by a sort of streusel, it more closely resembles cake than custard and is not prone to curdling.

Pecan Pie

One 9-inch pie; 8 servings

Made with white sugar and light corn syrup, the pecan pie has a mild, sweet, buttery flavor. For a dark pecan pie with a caramel-like taste, substitute light or dark brown sugar and/or dark corn syrup.

Building up a high fluted rim to hold all the filling, prepare in a 9-inch pie pan, preferably glass, glazing with the egg yolk:

Baked Flaky Pastry Crust, 22, or Pat-in-the-Pan Butter Crust, 26

Position a rack in the center of the oven. Preheat the oven to 375°F. Spread on a baking sheet:

2 cups pecans, coarsely chopped

Toast the nuts in the oven, stirring occasionally, until golden and fragrant, 6 to 10 minutes. Whisk until blended:

3 large eggs

1 cup sugar

1 cup light corn syrup

5 tablespoons unsalted butter, melted

1 teaspoon vanilla or 1 tablespoon dark rum

½ teaspoon salt

Stir in the toasted nuts. Warm the pie crust in the oven until it is hot to the touch, then immediately pour in the filling. Bake until the edges are firm and the center seems set but quivery, like gelatin, when the pan is nudged, 35 to 45 minutes. Let cool on a rack for at least 1½ hours before slicing. Serve the pie warm or at room temperature with:

Whipped Cream, 76, or vanilla ice cream

The pie can be made up to 2 days ahead. Store in the refrigerator, but let warm to room temperature or warm in a 275°F oven for 15 minutes before serving.

CHOCOLATE PECAN PIE

Chop 6 ounces bittersweet or semi-sweet chocolate; melt in the top of a double boiler over barely simmering water, or microwave on medium for 1½ to 2 minutes. Prepare *Pecan Pie, above,* decreasing the corn syrup to ½ cup and the butter to 1 tablespoon. Whisk one quarter of the filling into the melted chocolate, then blend the result into the remaining filling. Stir in the nuts. Proceed as directed. Bake until the edges of the pie are slightly puffed and the center seems set but still soft, 25 to 30 minutes.

CHOCOLATE CHIP OR CHUNK PECAN PIE

This pie is softer and lighter in texture than Chocolate Pecan Pie but even richer.

Prepare *Pecan Pie, above,* decreasing the pecans to 1 cup and stirring in 1 cup chocolate chips or 2 ounces each dark, milk, and white chocolate, cut into ¼-inch chunks, along with the nuts. Bake as directed. Refrigerate the pie until cold and hard, then slice. Before serving, warm the slices in a 275°F oven until the chocolate just begins to soften.

Chess Pie

One 9-inch pie; 8 servings

Egg yolks give this filling a sparkling translucency and a smooth, soft, and melting texture.

Prepare in a 9-inch pie pan, glazing with the egg yolk:

Baked Flaky Pastry Crust, 22

Position a rack in the center of the oven. Preheat the oven to 275°F. Warm the pie crust in the oven while you prepare the filling. Whisk in a heatproof bowl just until no yellow streaks remain:

1 large egg

4 large egg yolks

⅔ cup sugar

⅔ cup firmly packed light brown sugar

½ teaspoon salt

Whisk in:

⅔ cup light cream or evaporated milk, or ⅓ cup milk and ⅓ cup heavy cream

Scatter over the top:

6 tablespoons (¾ stick) unsalted butter, cut into small pieces

Bring 1 inch of water to a simmer in a skillet. Set the bowl in the skillet and gently whisk the mixture until shiny and warm to the touch. Stir in:

½ to ¾ cup chopped walnuts or pecans, toasted (optional)

Pour the filling into the crust. You now have two options. For a pie without meringue, bake until the edges are firm and the center looks set but quivery, like gelatin, when the pan is gently nudged, 50 to 65 minutes. For a pie with a meringue, as soon as the pie goes into the oven, measure out all the ingredients (and prepare the cornstarch paste) for:

Soft Meringue Topping, 31

Bake the pie just until the center resembles corn syrup in consistency when the pan is nudged, 25 to 40 minutes. Remove the pie from the oven, increase the oven temperature to 325°F, and proceed at once to finish the meringue. Spread a band of meringue around the edges of the pie, where the filling is firmest, anchoring the meringue to the crust at all points. Drop the remaining meringue in dollops over the center of the filling and gently spread it to make a smooth, cohesive topping. Return the meringue-topped pie to the oven and bake for 20 minutes. Let cool completely on a rack before slicing. Store the pie in the refrigerator for up to 3 days but bring it to room temperature before serving. If you have not topped the pie with meringue, you may wish to accompany it with:

Whipped Cream, 76

BUTTERMILK CHESS PIE

To some Southerners, this is the only true chess pie.

Prepare *Chess Pie, above,* substituting ⅔ cup additional granulated sugar for the brown sugar and ⅔ cup buttermilk for the light cream. Stir ½ cup *each* chopped raisins and chopped pecans or walnuts into the filling.

LEMON CHESS PIE

Lemon Chess Pie filling tastes very much like lemon curd.

Prepare *Chess Pie, above,* but substitute ⅔ cup additional granulated sugar for the brown sugar, the grated zest of 1 lemon for the salt, and ⅓ cup heavy cream plus ⅓ cup strained fresh lemon juice for the light cream or evaporated milk. Omit the nuts, or stir in ½ cup shredded sweetened dried coconut. Decrease the baking time to 25 to 40 minutes. If using a meringue, apply it after 10 to 15 minutes' baking.

JEFF DAVIS PIE

This is a spicy, fruited chess pie, usually topped with a meringue.

Prepare *Chess Pie, above,* adding ½ teaspoon ground cinnamon, ½ teaspoon freshly grated or ground nutmeg, and ⅛ teaspoon ground cloves to the egg mixture. Stir into the filling ½ cup *each* chopped dates, chopped raisins, and chopped toasted pecans or walnuts in place of the optional nuts.

Shoofly Pie

One 9-inch pie; 8 servings

There are both "dry-bottom" and "wet-bottom" versions of this Pennsylvania Dutch specialty. The former are almost like soft gingerbread in a crust, while the latter consist of a tender molasses custard topped with crumbs. This version is "wet."

Prepare in a 9-inch pie pan:

Baked Flaky Pastry Crust, 22, or Pat-in-the-Pan Butter Crust, 26

Position a rack in the center of the oven. Preheat the oven to 400°F. Combine in a bowl:

1 cup all-purpose flour

⅔ cup firmly packed dark brown sugar

5 tablespoons unsalted butter, softened

Mash with a fork or chop with a pastry blender until the mixture is crumbly. In a separate bowl, beat with a large spoon until thoroughly blended:

1 cup light molasses

1 large egg

1 teaspoon baking soda

Stir in thoroughly:

1 cup boiling water

Stir half of the crumb mixture into the molasses mixture and pour into the prepared crust. Sprinkle the remaining crumb mixture evenly over the top. Bake for 10 minutes. Reduce the oven temperature to 350°F and bake until the pie filling has puffed around the sides and feels firm in the center, 20 to 30 minutes more. Let cool completely on a rack before slicing. Store at room temperature for up to 3 days. Accompany with:

Whipped Cream, 76

ABOUT
CITRUS
PIES & TARTS

*T*hink of preparing these favorites when you're having company over—even on a weeknight—since all of the recipes in this chapter can be made ahead and refrigerated. Sweet, tart, and refreshing, lemon and lime pies and tarts make wonderful desserts.

If you are going to make a lemon or lime pie or tart from scratch, take the time to grate the zest and squeeze the juice from fresh citrus fruits. Citrus zest contains pungent oils essential to a delicious filling, and fresh juice tastes incomparably better than frozen or bottled. Remember that the lemon or lime juice isn't being used here to boost the flavor of another fruit in the recipe; it's the star of the show, and you want a pure, clean citrus flavor to burst forth in every mouth-watering bite.

Lemon Meringue Pie, 98

Lemon Meringue Pie

One 9-inch pie; 8 servings

Prepare in a 9-inch pie pan:

Baked Flaky Pastry Crust, 22, or a pat-in-the-pan crust, 26 to 29

Position a rack in the upper third of the oven. Preheat the oven to 325°F. Whisk thoroughly in a saucepan:

1¼ cups sugar

⅓ cup cornstarch

⅛ teaspoon salt

Whisk in, blending well:

1½ cups water

½ cup strained fresh lemon juice (from 2 to 3 lemons)

2 to 3 teaspoons grated lemon zest

Whisk in until no yellow streaks remain:

4 large egg yolks

Add:

2 to 3 tablespoons unsalted butter, cut into small pieces

Stirring constantly with a wooden spoon or rubber spatula, bring the mixture to a simmer over medium heat, then cook for 1 minute. The filling should be very thick. Pour the filling into the pie crust and press a sheet of plastic wrap directly on the surface. Immediately prepare:

Soft Meringue Topping, 31

Remove the plastic wrap from the pie and spread the meringue on top, anchoring the meringue to the edge of the crust at all points. Bake for 20 minutes. Let cool completely on a rack, then refrigerate. The pie can be stored for up to 3 days in the refrigerator. Serve at room temperature or cold.

Ohio Lemon Pie

One 9-inch pie; 8 servings

This pie (opposite) is often associated with the Shakers, a nineteenth-century religious group, though it was popular among all Americans by the time the Shakers adopted it. The filling consists of whole lemons, including the white pith, sliced paper-thin and macerated in sugar until tender and sweet. Before beginning, please read the material on pages 34 to 35.

Prepare:

Flaky Pastry Dough, 15, or Deluxe Butter Flaky Pastry Dough, 17

Roll half the dough into a 13-inch round, fit it into a 9-inch pie pan, and trim the overhanging dough to ¾ inch all around. Refrigerate. Roll the other half into a 12-inch round for the top crust and refrigerate it. Grate the zest from:

2 large or medium lemons

Slice the lemons paper-thin, removing the seeds as you do so. In a glass or stainless-steel bowl, combine the lemon slices and grated zest with:

2 cups sugar

¼ teaspoon salt

Cover and let stand at room temperature for 2 to 24 hours, stirring occasionally. The longer the lemons macerate, the better.

Position a rack in the lower third of the oven. Preheat the oven to 425°F. Whisk until frothy:

4 large eggs

Whisk in:

4 tablespoons (½ stick) butter, melted

3 tablespoons all-purpose flour

Stir the lemon mixture into the egg mixture. Pour the filling into the bottom crust and level with the back of a spoon. Brush the overhanging bottom crust with cold water. Cover with the top crust, trim, and crimp or flute the edge. Cut steam vents in the top crust. Bake the pie for 30 minutes. Reduce the oven temperature to 350°F and bake until the top crust has puffed and a knife inserted into the center comes out clean, 20 to 30 minutes more. Let cool completely on a rack. The pie can be stored in the refrigerator for up to 2 days, but let it warm to room temperature before serving.

Key Lime Pie

One 9-inch pie; 8 servings

If you do find the smaller, round Key limes, you may need as many as a dozen to yield ½ cup of juice. Either a whipped-cream or a meringue topping is an option here.

Prepare in a 9-inch pie pan:

Baked Flaky Pastry Crust, 22, or Crumb Crust, 30, made with graham crackers and baked

Position a rack in the center of the oven. Preheat the oven to 325°F. Whisk together until well blended:

One 15-ounce can sweetened condensed whole, low-fat, or skim milk

4 large egg yolks

½ cup strained fresh lime juice (from 3 to 4 limes)

3 to 4 teaspoons grated lime zest

The mixture will thicken as the milk reacts with the acidic citrus juice. Pour the filling into the pie crust. For a pie without a meringue topping, bake the pie until the center looks set but still quivery, like gelatin, when the pan is nudged, 15 to 17 minutes. Let cool completely on a rack, then refrigerate until cold or for up to 1 day. Shortly before serving, whip until thickened:

¾ cup cold heavy cream

Add:

¼ cup powdered sugar

Whip until stiff peaks form. Spread the whipped cream over the pie and serve.

For a pie with a meringue topping, let the unbaked pie stand at room temperature while you measure the ingredients (and prepare the cornstarch paste) for:

Soft Meringue Topping, 31

Bake the pie until the filling thickens just enough to support the topping, 5 to 7 minutes, but no longer. Meanwhile, finish the meringue. Spread a band of meringue around the edges of the filling, anchoring it to the crust at all points. Dollop the remaining meringue over the center and smooth the top. Bake for 20 minutes more. Let cool completely on a rack, then refrigerate until cold or for up to 1 day.

Lemon Angel Pie

One 10-inch pie; 8 servings

Position a rack in the center of the oven. Preheat the oven to 275°F. Using solid vegetable shortening, very generously grease the inside *and the rim* of a 10-inch pie pan, preferably glass. Dust the pan with flour, tilt to coat, then tap out the excess. In a large bowl, beat on medium speed until soft peaks form:

½ cup egg whites (about 4 large whites)
1 teaspoon vanilla (optional)
½ teaspoon cream of tartar

Very gradually add 1 tablespoon at a time, beating on high speed:

1 cup superfine sugar

Beat until the meringue holds very stiff peaks. Spread the meringue in the prepared pie pan, bringing the rim of the shell ½ inch higher than the pan. Bake the shell for 1 hour, then let cool on a rack.

In the top of a double boiler, whisk:

4 large egg yolks
½ cup sugar

Beat in:

2 to 3 teaspoons grated lemon zest
¼ cup strained fresh lemon juice

Set the pan over (not in) barely simmering water. Stirring gently, cook the mixture until thickened and stiff enough to mound softly on a spoon, 7 to 10 minutes. Place the top pan in cold water and, stirring now and then, let cool.

Beat on medium high speed until the peaks are stiff:

1 cup cold heavy cream

Fold ⅓ of the whipped cream into the lemon mixture, then gently fold in the remaining. Spread the filling in the meringue shell, press a sheet of plastic wrap directly on the surface, and refrigerate for 24 to 48 hours. No more than 8 hours before serving, beat on medium-high speed until thickened:

1 cup cold heavy cream

Gradually add and beat until the peaks are stiff:

½ cup powdered sugar

Spread over the top of the pie. If you wish, decorate or serve the pie with:

1 to 2 cups raspberries or blueberries

Lemon Tart

One 9½- or 10-inch tart; 8 servings

Prepare in a 9½- or 10-inch two-piece tart pan, glazing with the egg yolk:

Baked Flaky Pastry Crust, 22, made with Deluxe Butter Flaky Pastry Dough or Sweet Flaky Pastry Dough, 17, or Shortbread Crust, 28

Position a rack in the center of the oven. Preheat the oven to 350°F. Combine in a heatproof bowl:

1 cup sugar
8 tablespoons (1 stick) unsalted butter, cut into small pieces

Bring 1 inch of water to a bare simmer in a skillet. Set the bowl in the skillet and stir until the butter is melted. Remove the bowl from the skillet. Add and beat until no yellow streaks remain:

8 large egg yolks

Stir in:

½ cup strained fresh lemon juice (from 2 to 3 lemons)

Return the bowl to the skillet and, stirring gently, heat the mixture until thickened to the consistency of heavy cream (lightly coats a spoon), 6 to 8 minutes. Strain the lemon mixture through a clean fine-mesh sieve into a bowl, then stir in:

1 tablespoon grated lemon zest

Pour the filling into the tart crust. Bake the tart until the center looks set but still very quivery, like gelatin, when the pan is nudged, 15 to 20 minutes. If overbaked, the tart will be grainy around the edges. Let cool completely on a rack. Lightly oil a sheet of plastic wrap and press it directly on the filling. The tart can be stored in the refrigerator for up to 1 day. Let warm to room temperature before serving. If you wish, accompany with:

Fresh Raspberry Sauce, below

Fresh Raspberry Sauce

About 1 cup; 6 to 8 servings

Puree in a blender:

1 pint raspberries, or 12 ounces frozen raspberries, thawed
3 tablespoons sugar
2 teaspoons strained fresh lemon juice

Strain through a fine-mesh sieve, pressing firmly with a rubber spatula. Taste, then stir in a little more sugar or lemon juice if needed. Serve at once, or cover and refrigerate for up to 3 days.

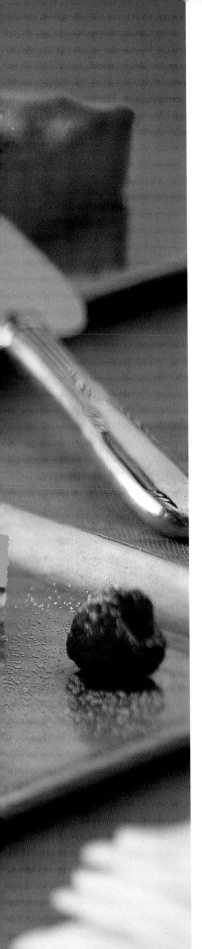

ABOUT
CHOCOLATE
PIES & TARTS

*T*he tarts in this section differ in their basic structure but are similar in their richness and intensity. For instance, Crustless Fudge Pie, 107, forms a crunchy border around the edges of the pie as it bakes, making a traditional crust unnecessary.

Besides chocolate, the filling of Bittersweet Chocolate Tart, 106, calls for only two other ingredients: a cup of cream and an egg. This tart has an utterly indulgent flavor and a silken texture. Reserve your best chocolate for this treat.

For the ultimate showstopper, prepare Chocolate-Glazed Caramel Tart, 105—a definite must for those who love caramel-filled chocolates. Top with toasted almonds and serve this elegant dessert for your next fancy dinner party.

Bittersweet Chocolate Tart, 106

Chocolate

Chocolate comes from almond-shaped beans that grow inside the pods of cacao trees in tropical areas near the equator. Cocoa beans, as they are known in the United States, develop their distinctive chocolate flavor, color, and aroma only after they have been fermented, dried, and roasted. To make chocolate, the roasted beans are chopped into small pieces called nibs. The nibs are rich in cocoa butter, a cream-colored, natural vegetable fat that melts during the grinding process producing a dark brown, fluid mass called chocolate liquor—the primary ingredient in all forms of chocolate except white.

Chocolate liquor, also known as unsweetened, bitter, baking, or cooking chocolate, is pure chocolate with no added ingredients. It contains nearly equal parts cocoa butter and cocoa solids, the meat of the cocoa bean, which is why it imparts such a deep, rich chocolate flavor. Unsweetened chocolate is combined with sugar in baking.

Extra-bittersweet, bittersweet, semisweet, and sweet chocolates are made of chocolate liquor, not more than 12 percent milk solids, cocoa butter, sugar, vanilla or vanillin, and lecithin. Bittersweet bars often have a deeper chocolate flavor than those labeled semisweet, and they are apt to be less sweet (although the amount of sugar they contain is not regulated). These chocolates may be

used interchangeably in most recipes, but their differences can alter the flavor, texture, and appearance of the finished product.

Chocolate-Glazed Caramel Tart

One 9½- or 10-inch tart; 10 to 12 servings

Prepare in a 9½- or 10-inch two-piece tart pan, glazing with the egg yolk:

Baked Flaky Pastry Crust, 22, or
Shortbread Crust, 28

Position a rack in the lower third of the oven. Preheat the oven to 325°F. Spread on a baking sheet:

½ cup slivered blanched almonds

Toast in the oven, stirring occasionally, until golden, 5 to 7 minutes. Let cool, then coarsely chop. Place in a medium, heavy saucepan:

1½ cups sugar

Drizzle evenly over the top:

½ cup water

Place the pan over medium heat and, without stirring, very gently swirl the pan by the handle until a clear syrup forms. It is important that the syrup clarify *before* the boil is reached, so slide the pan on and off the burner as necessary. Increase the heat to high and bring the syrup to a rolling boil. Cover the pan tightly and boil for 2 minutes. Uncover the pan and cook the syrup until it begins to darken. Once again gently swirl the pan and cook the syrup until it turns a deep amber. Remove the pan from the heat. Standing back to avoid possible spatters, pour in:

1¼ cups heavy cream

Stir until smooth. If the caramel remains lumpy, place the saucepan over low heat and stir until smooth. Let the mixture cool for 10 minutes. In a medium bowl, whisk until frothy:

1 large egg
1 large egg yolk

1 teaspoon vanilla
⅛ teaspoon salt

Gradually whisk in the caramel mixture. Pour the filling into the prepared tart crust and bake until the edges darken and begin to bubble and the center looks almost set, 45 to 55 minutes. Let cool completely on a rack. Heat in the top of a double boiler over gently simmering water until melted and smooth:

3 ounces bittersweet or semisweet
chocolate, finely chopped
¼ cup heavy cream

Spread the chocolate glaze over the caramel filling and sprinkle with the toasted almonds. Refrigerate the tart until firm or for up to 2 days. Serve cold with:

Whipped Cream, 76

Bittersweet Chocolate Tart

One 9½- or 10-inch tart; 8 to 10 servings

Prepare in a 9½- or 10-inch two-piece tart pan:

Shortbread Crust, 28

Position a rack in the lower third of the oven. Preheat the oven to 375°F. In a small saucepan, bring to a simmer:

1 cup heavy cream

Remove from the heat and add:

8 ounces bittersweet or semisweet chocolate, finely chopped

Whisk until the chocolate is completely melted and the mixture is smooth, then whisk in:

1 large egg, lightly beaten

Pour the chocolate mixture into the tart shell. Bake until the center seems set but still quivery, like gela-tin, when the pan is nudged, 15 to 18 minutes. Let cool on a rack. Serve slightly warm or at room temperature with:

Whipped Cream, 76

The tart is best served the day it is baked but it can be refrigerated for 2 to 3 days. Let warm to room temperature before serving.

HOW TO SHAVE AND MELT CHOCOLATE

Shaved chocolate is often used to decorate chocolate pies and tarts. Melted chocolate is used to make fillings. Containers and stirring utensils used for melting chocolate must be clean and dry; do not let stray drops of water touch the chocolate. Small amounts of water may cause melted chocolate to lose its gloss and tighten or "seize."

1 To shave chocolate, warm it by setting it in a warm place or stroking it with your palm. Scrape the blade of a paring knife or vegetable peeler across it at a 45 degree angle.

2 To melt chocolate, first chop it into pieces with a sharp, dry knife.

3 To melt chocolate using a water bath, place one-third of it in the top of a double boiler or in a bowl that fits snugly over the top of a saucepan. Fill the bottom pan with enough hot tap water (130°F) to touch the bottom of the top bowl, but not so much as to allow the bowl to float. Avoid splashing water into it. Begin stirring with a rubber spatula when the outside edges of the chocolate begin to liquefy. Gradually add the rest of the chocolate. Carefully lift the bowl of chocolate from the water bath when the chocolate is nearly melted, dry the bottom, and continue stirring the chocolate until it is smooth and shiny.

To melt chocolate using the microwave, select a dry, microwave-safe plastic bowl and fill it no more than half full with chopped chocolate. Microwave 1 to 8 ounces of dark chocolate, uncovered, on medium power for 1½ minutes to 3½ minutes, depending on the amount of chocolate. Use low power for milk and white chocolates. Stir the chocolate with a rubber spatula after the first 1½ minutes, even if it appears firm. If necessary, continue microwaving in increasingly shorter increments at the appropriate power level until most of the chocolate is melted. Stir until the chocolate is smooth and shiny.

Crustless Fudge Pie

One 9-inch pie; 8 to 10 servings

This superb confection has appeared in JOY since our 1943 edition. We call it a pie because it forms a sort of crust around the sides during baking, but it could just as aptly be considered a fudgy brownie or dense chocolate cake. It is devastatingly rich, but do not let that deter you.

Position a rack in the center of the oven. Preheat the oven to 325°F. Generously butter a 9-inch pie pan. Sprinkle the inside with flour, tilt the pan in all directions to coat, and tap out the excess.

Stirring from time to time, melt in the top of a double boiler over barely simmering water or in a microwave on medium power (opposite):

2 ounces unsweetened chocolate, finely chopped

Let cool. In a medium bowl, cream with the back of a wooden spoon until fluffy:

1 cup sugar

8 tablespoons (1 stick) unsalted butter, softened

Beat in the chocolate along with:

2 large egg yolks

1 teaspoon vanilla

Stir just until blended:

⅓ cup all-purpose flour

Fold in:

1 cup coarsely chopped walnuts or pecans

In a separate bowl, beat on medium-high speed until foamy:

2 large egg whites, at room temperature

Add:

⅛ teaspoon of cream of tartar

Increase the speed to high and beat until the peaks are stiff but not dry. Using a rubber spatula, fold the egg whites into the chocolate mixture. Spread the batter evenly in the prepared pan and bake until the center feels almost firm when gently pressed, 25 to 35 minutes. Let cool completely on a rack before slicing. Serve the pie warm or at room temperature with:

Whipped Cream, 76, or vanilla ice cream

The pie can be stored, loosely covered, at room temperature for up to 1 day. If you wish, warm it in a 300°F oven for about 10 minutes before serving.

ABOUT
SAVORY
PIES & TARTS

*T*hese savory pies and tarts are sure to become family favoites. They also make great dishes to bring to potluck parties because they are easy to transport and reheat.

From casual to elegant to hearty, these savory dishes are extremely versatile to serve. Cut large tarts into bite-sized pieces for hors d'oeuvres. Pair a wedge of savory tart with a simple tossed salad for a sophisticated lunch. For a simple evening meal with family and friends, serve a meaty pot pie.

You'll notice that many of these recipes use crusts that you mastered for sweet pies. Some have their own doughs. All lend themselves to experimentation when it comes to their fillings. Try swapping the ground beef in the Empanadas, 114, with ground turkey or even black beans. Toss some roasted red peppers or sautéed onions into the mixture for Pizza Rustica, 117. Adapt these recipes to meet your family's tastes and to vary them from time to time.

Quiche Lorraine, 110

Quiche Lorraine

One 9-inch quiche; 4 to 6 servings

This brunch and lunch classic is a specialty of the Lorraine region of northeastern France, where it was first made as early as the sixteenth century. Traditional quiche Lorraine contains no cheese. For a more elegant presentation, it can also be baked as individual tartlets.

Preheat the oven to 375°F.

Prepare and bake in a 9½- or 10-inch two-piece tart pan and glaze with egg yolk:

Flaky Pastry Dough, 15

Cook in a heavy skillet over medium heat, stirring constantly, until the fat is almost rendered but the bacon is not yet crisp:

4 ounces sliced bacon, cut into 1-inch pieces

Drain the bacon on paper towels. Beat together:

3 large eggs, lightly beaten
1½ cups crème fraîche, heavy cream, or half cream and half milk
½ teaspoon salt
¼ teaspoon ground black pepper
Pinch of freshly grated or ground nutmeg

Arrange the bacon on the bottom of the shell and pour the custard over it. Bake until the filling is browned and set, 25 to 35 minutes.

HAM AND CHEESE QUICHE

Prepare *Quiche Lorraine, left,* substituting 1 cup chopped ham for the cooked bacon and spreading 1 cup grated Gruyère or other cheese on the bottom of the pie shell before adding the custard.

BROCCOLI QUICHE

Sauté ½ red onion, chopped, and 1 clove garlic, minced, in olive oil until soft. Blanch and drain ⅔ cup broccoli florets. Prepare *Quiche Lorraine, left,* omitting the bacon. Spread the onions and broccoli, and ¾ cup grated Gruyère or other cheese on the bottom of the pie shell before adding the custard.

Leek Tart (Flamiche aux Poireaux)

One 9-inch tart; 6 servings

This is a rich leek and cream pie from northern France.

Prepare:

½ recipe Flaky Pastry Dough, 15, or Deluxe Butter Flaky Pastry Dough, 17

Roll out the dough ⅛ inch thick and fit into a buttered 9-inch quiche, tart, or pie pan. Refrigerate while you prepare the filling.

Melt in a medium skillet over medium heat:

2 tablespoons unsalted butter

Add:

2 pounds leeks, trimmed to white and tender green parts only, split lengthwise, cleaned thoroughly, and cut into ¼-inch-thick slices (about 4 cups)
½ teaspoon salt
Ground black pepper to taste

Cover and cook until the leeks are very soft, with little color, stirring occasionally and reducing the heat as they cook, about 30 minutes. After about 15 minutes of cooking time, set a rack in the lowest position in the oven. Preheat the oven to 400°F.

Beat together until well combined:

2 large eggs
½ cup heavy cream, half-and-half, or light cream
¼ teaspoon freshly grated or ground nutmeg
Salt and ground black pepper to taste

Remove the pastry shell from the refrigerator. When the leeks are done, add to the custard and transfer to the prepared pastry shell. Bake until golden and the custard is set, 20 to 30 minutes. Let rest for 10 minutes to settle (opposite), then cut into wedges and serve.

LEEKS

Looking like enormous scallions with flat rather than hollow leaves, leeks are an ancient member of the onion family, milder and sweeter than any others in the clan. When buying a bunch, be sure the leaves are bright, crisp, and not torn, and the white parts are not discolored. Store in perforated plastic vegetable bags in the refrigerator crisper.

The layers of a leek can contain dirt, since the white stalks are "blanched," buried in earth to keep them pale. Swish julienned or sliced leeks in a large bowl of cool water. Let them stand a few minutes while the dirt falls to the bottom, then lift them out with a strainer. Repeat if there is a lot of dirt left in the bowl.

Tomato and Fontina Cheese Tart

One 9-inch pie or 10-inch tart; 6 to 8 servings

Serve in thin wedges as an appetizer or as a meatless main dish.

Preheat the oven to 400°F.

Combine in a large bowl:

1 ¾ cups all-purpose flour

¼ teaspoon salt

12 tablespoons (1½ sticks) cold butter, cut into small pieces

Work the butter into the flour with a pastry blender or your fingers until it resembles coarse crumbs. Stir in, bit by bit, just until the pastry comes together:

4 tablespoons ice water

Roll out the dough with a little flour into a 12-inch round, ⅛ inch thick. Fit into a 10-inch tart pan or a 9-inch pie plate. Brush the pastry with

¼ cup Dijon mustard

Cover with:

2 cups loosely packed shredded Fontina cheese

Layer over the cheese in overlapping, concentric circles,

8 medium tomatoes, thinly sliced

Sprinkle with:

1 tablespoon chopped garlic

2 teaspoons chopped fresh marjoram

2 teaspoons extra-virgin olive oil

Bake for 40 minutes and let cool slightly before serving.

Tomato and Goat Cheese Quiche

One 9-inch quiche; 6 servings

Prepare:

½ recipe Flaky Pastry Dough, 15, or Deluxe Butter Flaky Pastry Dough, 17

Roll out the dough ⅛ inch thick and fit into a buttered 9-inch quiche, tart, or pie pan. Refrigerate while you prepare the filling.

Set a rack in the lowest position in the oven. Preheat the oven to 400°F. Core, quarter lengthwise, seed, and set aside:

1 pound plum tomatoes (about 6)

Crumble into a bowl:

4 ounces fresh goat cheese

Slowly mash in until smooth:

¾ cup half-and-half or heavy cream

½ cup milk

Add and whisk until smooth:

3 large eggs

1 tablespoon chopped fresh parsley

1½ teaspoons chopped fresh thyme or savory or 3 tablespoons chopped fresh basil

¼ teaspoon salt

Plenty of ground black pepper

Remove the pastry shell from the refrigerator and arrange the tomato quarters in the shell like the spokes of a wheel, with the pointed end (blossom end) toward the center of the quiche. Fill in the center with more tomato quarters. Pour the cheese mixture over the tomatoes and bake until the pastry and top are golden brown, 40 to 45 minutes. Let the quiche rest for 10 minutes to settle, then cut into wedges and serve.

Chard Tart

One 11-inch tart; 6 to 8 servings

A springtime tradition in many parts of Italy and France. Escarole leaves, spinach, or other spring vegetables can be mixed in or substituted for the chard.

Position a rack in the lower third of the oven. Preheat the oven to 425°F. To prepare the pastry, whisk together in a medium bowl:

1¾ cups all-purpose flour

¾ teaspoon salt

Stir in with a fork until thoroughly blended:

½ cup extra-virgin olive oil

⅓ cup cold milk or water

The dough will be very crumbly and difficult to roll, so press it evenly into an 11-inch tart pan with a removable rim. Bake until the crust is set and lightly golden, 10 to 15 minutes, pricking the bottom once or twice if it bubbles. Meanwhile, cook in a large skillet over medium-low heat until well softened, stirring occasionally, 10 to 15 minutes:

2 tablespoons olive oil

1 red onion, finely diced

Increase the heat to medium and add and cook until tender, 8 to 10 minutes:

1 pound chard leaves or other greens, stems removed, leaves well washed and chopped

2 cloves garlic, chopped

Season with:

2 tablespoons chopped fresh basil, or 1½ teaspoons dried, finely crumbled

¼ teaspoon salt

⅛ teaspoon ground black pepper

Pinch of ground red pepper, or to taste

Combine in a bowl:

3 large eggs, lightly beaten

⅓ cup heavy cream or half-and-half

1 cup grated Parmesan cheese

Add the chard mixture, then scrape the mixture into the prepared tart shell and spread evenly. Reduce the oven to 375°F. Bake until the filling is golden and firm, 25 to 35 minutes. Let cool to room temperature before serving.

CHARD

When you see the large, ruffled, rich green leaves of Swiss chard at the market, you might imagine they have a flamboyant flavor to match. In fact, chard has a more delicate taste than spinach, and very young chard leaves are as mild as lettuce. The *Swiss* is a puzzlement; there is nothing Swiss about this close relative of beets. But there is more to this vegetable than leaves. The fleshy ribs can be prepared separately; they taste like earthy celery. Chard leaves may be green with white ribs or burgundy with crimson ribs. Select the bunch with the smallest, crispest, brightest leaves and no yellowing, tears, or holes. Store in perforated plastic vegetable bags in the refrigerator crisper.

Empanadas

10 to 12 large empanadas

These flaky meat pies are a much-loved snack all through Latin America. Although they can be filled with anything from fish to fruit, a meat filling is most common. Lard makes the most flavorful, flaky crust, but solid vegetable shortening is certainly acceptable.

For the dough, place in a large bowl or food processor:

3 cups all-purpose flour
1½ teaspoons baking powder
1 teaspoon salt

Mix with a fork or pulse until combined. Add:

10 tablespoons (1¼ sticks) cold
unsalted butter, cut into small
pieces
½ cup lard or solid vegetable
shortening, cut into small pieces

Cut the butter and lard into the flour mixture using a pastry blender or pulse in the food processor until the mixture resembles coarse crumbs. If using the food processor, transfer the mixture to a large bowl. Drizzle over the top:

11 to 13 tablespoons ice water

Mix gently with a fork until the flour mixture is dampened enough to gather into a ball. Shape into a thick, flat disk, wrap tightly in plastic, and refrigerate for at least 1 hour. For the filling, heat in a large nonstick skillet over medium heat:

1 tablespoon vegetable oil

Add:

1 medium onion, diced
2 cloves garlic, minced

Cook, stirring, until the onion is translucent, about 5 minutes. Stir in:

1 pound lean ground beef

Cook until the beef is lightly browned, about 8 minutes. Stir in:

1 cup diced peeled potatoes
1 large tomato, cored and chopped
¼ cup raisins (optional)
¼ cup coarsely chopped pitted
green olives (optional)
1 teaspoon dried oregano
½ teaspoon salt
½ teaspoon ground black pepper
¼ teaspoon dried thyme

Cook, covered, over medium heat until the potatoes are tender, about

10 minutes. Uncover the pan, increase the heat to medium-high, and cook briefly to evaporate any pan juices. Remove from the heat and let cool completely.

Preheat the oven to 400°F.

To shape the empanadas, roll out the dough ⅛ inch thick on a lightly floured surface. Cut 6-inch rounds from the dough. (You will have to reroll the scraps to get 10 to 12 rounds.) Spoon about ¼ cup of the filling onto one side of each round. Moisten the edges of the rounds with water, fold each one in half, and press the edges together to completely enclose the filling. Use the tines of a fork to decoratively seal the edges. Place 2 inches apart on a baking sheet. Mix together and brush over the tops of the empanadas:

1 large egg, lightly beaten
1 tablespoon milk
Pinch of salt

Bake until nicely browned, about 15 minutes. Let cool slightly on a rack and serve warm.

Tamale Pie

8 to 10 servings

Unlike many tamale pies, which have a top crust only, this one is completely enclosed in a cornmeal crust (opposite).

Crumble into a large skillet and cook over medium-high heat until the meat is no longer pink, thoroughly breaking up the meat with the back of a spoon:

1½ pounds lean ground beef or ground turkey

If necessary, tilt the skillet and spoon out any fat. Stir in:

3 cups tomato salsa

½ cup chopped pimiento-stuffed green olives

1 tablespoon chili powder

1 tablespoon ground cumin

½ teaspoon ground cinnamon

Bring the mixture to a simmer. Reduce the heat to low and simmer gently, stirring occasionally, for 10 minutes. Remove from the heat. Bring just to a boil in a small saucepan:

1⅓ cups water

1 cup vegetable or chicken stock

Cover and remove from the heat. Whisk together in a large bowl:

2 teaspoons baking powder

1½ teaspoons salt

Whisk in:

⅓ cup vegetable oil

Then stir in, mixing until all the cornmeal is coated with the oil:

3 cups yellow cornmeal

Add the reserved stock mixture and stir well. Let the batter stand for 5 minutes. Mix in:

2 large eggs

Position a rack in the center of the oven. Preheat the oven to 400°F.

Generously grease a 13 x 9-inch baking dish, preferably glass. Remove 1½ cups of the cornmeal batter and reserve. Using a rubber spatula, spread the remaining batter evenly over the bottom and all the way up the sides of the pan. Gently spoon the beef filling over the crust, then cover evenly with:

12 ounces grated sharp Cheddar cheese (about 3 packed cups)

Stir into the reserved batter:

¼ cup hot water

Then spread it in a thin, even layer over the top of the pie. The batter will blend lightly with the cheese. Bake the pie until nicely browned, about 40 minutes. Let stand for 15 minutes. Cut the pie lengthwise in half, then cut each half crosswise into 4 or 5 equal pieces.

Pizza Rustica (Italian Meat Pie)

Sixteen 2-inch square servings

The flavor of this pizza is best when served cold.

Preheat the oven to 400°F. To prepare the filling, beat together until smooth:

2 pounds ricotta cheese

4 large eggs

Add and mix well:

8 ounces sweet Italian sausage, baked or fried, cooled, and coarsely chopped

8 ounces pork fillet or any other lean pork meat, cut into small cubes, fried, and cooled

8 ounces mozzarella cheese, cut into small cubes

4 ounces prosciutto, diced

½ cup grated Parmesan cheese

¼ cup finely chopped fresh Italian parsley

Ground black pepper to taste

To prepare the pie crust, on a pastry board or in a bowl, combine:

2 cups sifted all-purpose flour

¼ cup sugar

2 teaspoons baking powder

With your fingers, break into the flour until the flour is mealy:

8 tablespoons (1 stick) butter

Make a well, and break into it:

2 large eggs

Beat the eggs with a fork. Blend into the flour mixture, knead quickly, and gather into a ball. Let rest for 10 minutes under a bowl. The dough will be soft and quite sticky.

Lightly flour about two-thirds of the dough and roll out to fit a 8 x 8 x 2-inch pan, with a ½-inch overhang. Pour the meat mixture into the pastry-lined pan. Roll out the remaining dough and cover the top. Trim the overhang and press the edges with the tines of a fork. Prick the top crust with the fork to allow steam to escape. If desired, brush the top with:

1 egg yolk, well beaten

Bake for 15 minutes. Reduce the oven temperature to 325°F and cook for 45 to 55 minutes more. Turn off the heat and let the pizza cool in the oven. Cut into 2-inch squares and serve warm or cold.

Greek Spinach and Cheese Pie (Spanakopita)

About thirty 2-inch squares or diamonds

For tiropetes, triangular-shaped, individual packets, spoon small mounds of the filling onto 3-inch-wide strips of phyllo. Fold up into triangles and bake for 15 to 20 minutes.

Stem, wash well, and coarsely chop:

2 pounds spinach

Heat in a large skillet over medium heat:

2 tablespoons olive oil

Add and cook until softened, 5 to 7 minutes:

1 large onion, finely chopped

4 scallions, finely chopped

Add the chopped spinach a handful at a time. Cook until the spinach is wilted and the liquid is released, 5 minutes. Increase the heat to high and cook, stirring often, until the liquid is evaporated and the spinach is dry, 7 to 10 minutes. Stir in:

¼ cup snipped fresh dill or chopped fresh parsley

Let stand until cool enough to handle, then squeeze to remove the excess liquid. In a medium bowl, lightly beat:

4 large eggs

Add the cooked spinach mixture along with:

8 ounces feta cheese, crumbled

2 tablespoons grated kefalotiri (Greek grating cheese) or Parmesan cheese

½ teaspoon salt

Several grinds of black pepper

Pinch of freshly grated or ground nutmeg

Lightly oil a 13 x 9-inch baking pan. Melt:

8 tablespoons (1 stick) butter

Unroll on a dry work surface:

1 pound phyllo dough, thawed if frozen

Trim 1 inch from the edges of the phyllo dough. Cover with a dry

towel and cover the dry towel with a damp towel. Lay 1 sheet of phyllo in and up the sides of the prepared pan and brush lightly with melted butter. Top with 7 more phyllo sheets, brushing each one lightly with butter. Spread the spinach mixture over the layered phyllo. Top with 8 more sheets, brushing each one with butter, including the top sheet. Roll the overhanging phyllo from the sides to form a border all the way around. With a thin, sharp knife, cut the pie into squares or diamonds, but do not cut through the bottom or the filling will leak onto the pan. Refrigerate for 30 minutes. Preheat the oven to 375°F. Bake the spinach pie until crisp and golden, about 45 minutes. Remove from the oven and let stand for a few minutes. Cut right through to the bottom and serve.

PHYLLO

Phyllo, literally *leaf* in Greek, can be made by hand, but we do not recommend it; it is an arduous and tricky process that yields results no better than what is commercially available frozen in most grocery stores or fresh from Greek and Middle Eastern bakeries. Store-bought phyllo is easy to work with, but it is essential to keep the thin sheets from drying out. If using frozen phyllo, thaw it slowly, without unwrapping, in the refrigerator for several hours or overnight. Once it is thawed, unwrap the phyllo and remove only the number of sheets required for the recipe; rewrap the remaining sheets in plastic wrap and return them to the refrigerator or freezer. Stack the sheets to be used on a tray or a sheet of plastic wrap, cover the stack with a sheet of plastic wrap, and cover the wrap with a damp towel. (Do not allow the damp towel to touch the phyllo, or it will dissolve into paste.) A sheet of phyllo left uncovered dries out in just a minute and will crack when you try to use it. Remove from the covered stack only the number of sheets of phyllo immediately called for and quickly re-cover the stack before proceeding.

Chicken or Turkey Pot Pie

6 to 8 servings

This pot pie has a top crust only, which may be either biscuit or pie pastry. Sautéing the vegetables separately instead of cooking them with the chicken ensures that they will retain their texture and color. This recipe includes directions for poaching raw poultry. You can also use 4 cups diced or shredded skinless cooked poultry. Just substitute 2 cups canned chicken broth for the reserved poaching broth.

3½ pounds chicken parts or 1½ pounds boneless, skinless chicken breast or turkey breast cutlets or tenders

Place the chicken in a Dutch oven. Add:

1¾ to 2 cups chicken stock

Pour in just enough water to cover the pieces. Chicken parts may require as much as 3 cups water to be covered, while boneless, skinless breasts may not need any at all. Bring to a simmer over high heat,

then reduce the heat so that the poaching liquid barely bubbles. Partially cover and cook until the meat releases clear juices when pierced with a fork, 25 to 30 minutes for chicken parts, 8 to 12 minutes for boneless, skinless chicken or turkey breast. Remove the meat from the stock and let stand until cool enough to handle. If using chicken parts, remove and discard the skin and bones. Cut or shred the meat into bite-sized pieces. Skim the fat from the stock with a spoon. Melt in a large saucepan over medium-low heat:

4 tablespoons (½ stick) unsalted butter

Add and whisk until smooth:

½ cup all-purpose flour

Cook, whisking constantly, for 1 minute. Remove the pan from the heat. Add 2 cups of the chicken stock and whisk until smooth. Whisk in:

1½ cups whole milk, half-and-half, or light cream

Increase the heat to medium and bring the mixture just to a simmer, whisking constantly. Remove the pan from the heat, scrape the inside of the saucepan with a wooden spoon or heatproof rubber spatula, and whisk vigorously to break up any lumps. Return the pan to the heat and, whisking, bring to a simmer and cook for 1 minute. Stir in the cooked poultry along with:

2 to 3 tablespoons sherry (optional)

Cook for 1 minute. Remove from the heat and season to taste with:

Several drops of lemon juice

Salt and ground white or black pepper

2 to 3 pinches of freshly grated or ground nutmeg

Prepare:

Basic Biscuit Dough, 122, ½ recipe Flaky Pastry Dough, 15, or ½ recipe Deluxe Butter Flaky Pastry Dough, 17

Refrigerate the biscuit or pastry dough.

Position a rack in the upper third of the oven. Preheat the oven to 400°F. Butter a 13 x 9-inch baking pan or other shallow baking dish.

Heat in a large skillet over medium-high heat until the foam begins to subside:

2 tablespoons unsalted butter

Add and cook, stirring often, until barely tender, about 5 minutes:

1 medium onion, chopped

3 medium carrots, peeled and sliced ¼ inch thick

2 small celery stalks, sliced ¼ inch thick

Stir the vegetables into the creamed chicken along with:

¾ cup frozen peas, thawed

3 tablespoons minced fresh parsley

Pour the chicken mixture into the prepared pan. If using biscuit dough, for rolled biscuits, roll out the dough ½ inch thick, then cut into 2-inch rounds and arrange on top of the chicken, overlapping the biscuits if necessary; for drop biscuits, simply drop small biscuits on the top. If using pie dough, roll it out into the shape of the pan, place on top of the chicken, and tuck the edges in against the pan sides. For a golden brown glaze, brush the top with:

2 tablespoons beaten egg (½ large)

Bake until the chicken is bubbly and the topping is nicely browned, 25 to 35 minutes.

Vegetable Pot Pie with Cheddar Biscuit Crust

8 to 12 servings

This dish makes wonderful party food because it serves a crowd and the vegetables can be prepared up to 1 day ahead: Cut up, brown, and place the vegetables in the baking dish. The crust can be made up to 2 hours ahead and kept covered at room temperature. Keep the vegetables in large chunks as directed in the recipe so that they remain intact and do not cook down to a puree.

Prepare and keep each vegetable in separate bowls:

2 medium red onions (about 1 pound), cut into thick slices

3 medium carrots, peeled and cut into 1-inch pieces

3 parsnips, peeled and cut into 1-inch pieces

1 celery root, peeled and cut into 1-inch pieces

1 butternut squash (about 2½ pounds), peeled and cut into 1-inch pieces

1 acorn squash (about 1½ pounds), peeled and cut into 1-inch pieces

8 ounces portobello mushrooms, cut into thick slices and slices halved crosswise

Have ready:

3 or 4 tablespoons olive oil

3 or 4 tablespoons unsalted butter

Heat ½ tablespoon oil and ½ tablespoon butter in a large skillet over medium-high heat. Add the onion slices and cook until browned, about 3 minutes on each side. Transfer to a large bowl and season with:

Salt and ground black pepper to taste

Add a bit more oil and butter to the pan, then add the carrots and parsnips. Brown, stirring frequently, for 5 to 7 minutes, transfer to the bowl, and season with salt and pepper. Repeat, adding oil and butter as needed, with the celery root and squashes, browning them all separately and seasoning with salt and pepper as you place them in the bowl. Add the mushrooms to the pan with more oil and butter if needed, turn the heat to high, and brown them well, tossing frequently, about 5 to 7 minutes. Add to the bowl and season with salt and pepper. Preheat the oven to 400°F.

Add to the vegetables:

2 tablespoon chopped fresh marjoram, or 1 tablespoon dried

Gently mix the herb and vegetables together, transfer to a 13 x 9-inch baking dish, and spread evenly in 1 layer. Pour over the vegetables:

4 cups vegetable or chicken stock

Cover the dish and bake until the vegetables are just tender when pierced with the tip of a sharp knife, 30 to 45 minutes. While the vegetables bake, prepare:

1 recipe *Basic Biscuit Dough*, left

using heavy cream in place of the milk and adding with the cream:

¾ cup grated Cheddar cheese

2 teaspoons minced garlic (optional)

¼ teaspoon cracked black pepper

Set aside. After the vegetables have cooked for 30 to 45 minutes, uncover the dish and spoon dollops of biscuit dough over the vegetables (opposite). Continue baking until the biscuits are browned, 20 to 25 minutes more. Remove from the oven, let stand for 10 minutes, and serve.

Basic Biscuit Dough

About twenty biscuits

Whisk together thoroughly in a large bowl:

2 cups all-purpose flour

2½ teaspoons baking powder

½ to ¾ teaspoon salt

Drop in:

5 to 6 tablespoons cold unsalted butter, cut into pieces

Cut in the butter with 2 knives or a pastry blender, tossing the pieces with the flour mixture to coat and separate them as you work. For biscuits with crunchy edges and a flaky, layered structure, continue to cut in the butter until the largest pieces are the size of peas and the rest resemble breadcrumbs. For classic fluffy biscuits, continue to cut in the butter until the mixture resembles coarse breadcrumbs. Do not allow the butter to melt or form a paste with the flour.

Add all at once:

¾ cup milk

Mix with a rubber spatula, wooden spoon, or fork just until most of the dry ingredients are moistened. With a lightly floured hand, gather the dough into a ball and knead it gently against the sides and bottom of the bowl 5 to 10 times, turning and pressing any loose pieces into the dough each time until they adhere and the bowl is fairly clean.

Pasties

6 pasties

When the copper boom was at its peak in Michigan's Upper Peninsula in the 1800s, immigrants from Finland and England flooded the area to work in the mines. While the name "pasty" is originally from Cornwall, both groups baked their own version of pasty. The Finnish often used a thin rye crust stuffed with fish or rice. Ours is more reminiscent of the Cornish-style pasty. Both provided the miners with the perfect portable lunch.

Combine well:

1¼ pounds beef round steak, cut into ½-inch cubes, or ground chuck

2½ cups ½-inch cubes peeled rutabagas or turnips

2½ cups ½-inch cubes peeled potatoes

1 cup ½-inch cubes peeled carrots

2 medium onions, coarsely chopped

Salt and ground black pepper to taste

Cover and set aside. Mix together in a large bowl:

4 cups all-purpose flour

1 tablespoon sugar

½ teaspoon salt

Cut in with a pastry blender or 2 knives until the mixture resembles coarse crumbs:

1¾ cups solid vegetable shortening

Mix together:

½ cup water

1 large egg

1 tablespoon white vinegar

Add the liquid ingredients to the dry ingredients and mix just until combined. Turn out onto a floured work surface. Divide into 6 portions and roll out each to form an 8-inch round.

Preheat the oven to 400°F.

Divide the filling among the 6 rounds, spooning the filling onto half of each dough round. Fold the dough over the filling and tuck it under the filling. Moisten the exposed edge and bring it up to meet the tucked edge, pinching the dough together to seal it. (Each pasty should resemble a small football, flattened on the bottom side.) Cut a slit in the top of each pasty and place on an ungreased baking sheet. Bake until the crust is golden, 50 to 60 minutes. Serve warm or at room temperature.

Steak and Mushroom Pie

4 to 6 servings

This version of the English pub classic, steak and kidney pie, is made with mushrooms, whose rich and earthy flavor complements the beef.

Preheat the oven to 350°F.

Pat dry and cut into 2-inch pieces:

2 pounds beef round, rump, or chuck steak

Season with:

1 teaspoon salt

1 teaspoon ground black pepper

Dredge in:

½ cup all-purpose flour

Shake off the excess. Heat in a large skillet over high heat:

3 tablespoons butter, rendered beef fat, or vegetable oil

Add the meat in 2 batches and brown well on all sides, being careful not to crowd the pan, about 3 to 4 minutes. Remove the meat with a slotted spoon. Reduce the heat to medium. If the pan is dry, add:

2 tablespoons butter

Add and cook, stirring, until browned, about 2 minutes:

1 pound portobello, cremini, or white mushrooms, wiped clean and thickly sliced

Transfer to a plate and set aside.

Return the pan to medium heat. Add and cook until softened, about 3 minutes:

3 tablespoons butter

2 cups finely chopped onions

Pinch of salt

Pinch of ground black pepper

Pinch of dried thyme

Add and cook, stirring, until evenly incorporated:

3 tablespoons all-purpose flour

Add to the pan:

2 cups dry red wine or ale

1 cup beef stock

Bring to a boil, reduce the heat, and simmer until slightly thickened. Butter an 8- to 10-inch ovenproof casserole with a 2- to 3-quart capacity. Spoon the meat into the bottom and cover with the mushrooms. Pour the thickened stock and onion mixture over all. Bake, covered, for 1 to 1½ hours. Taste and adjust the seasonings. If desired, add:

¼ cup chopped fresh parsley

2 tablespoons snipped fresh chives

Cool completely. At this point, the filling can be refrigerated for up to 2 days.

To finish the pie, preheat the oven to 425°F.

Roll out and cover the filling in the casserole with:

½ recipe *Deluxe Butter Flaky Pastry Dough*, 17, or the dough for *Basic Rolled Biscuits*, 122

Whisk together and brush lightly over the top of the dough:

1 large egg

2 tablespoons milk

Bake until the pastry is golden and fully cooked, 25 to 30 minutes. Serve at once.

MUSHROOMS

Mushrooms lend both elegance and earthiness to a dish. While we are grateful for the abundance of cultivated small button mushrooms, wild mushrooms have considerably more character, and an assortment of them is available in specialty groceries and supermarkets. Choose mushrooms that are heavy for their size, with dry, firm caps and stems—nothing damp or shriveled, no dark or soft spots, and all close to the same size. If the gills are open, the mushrooms are more mature and their flavor will be stronger, and with a wild mushroom, this may be a plus. Open-gilled mushrooms should be used as soon as possible. A trick: When a costly mushroom is needed to flavor a dish, buy one or two, depending on the intensity of its flavor, then fill in with neutral-tasting button mushrooms.

Index

Bold type indicates that a recipe has an accompanying photograph.

Acknowledgments

Special thanks to my wife and editor in residence, Susan; and our friends and agents, Gene Winick and Sam Pinkus. Much appreciation also goes to Simon & Schuster, Scribner, and Weldon Owen for their devotion to this project. Thank you Carolyn, Susan, Beth, Rica, Bill, Marah, John, Terry, Roger, Gaye, Val, and all the other capable and talented folks who gave a part of themselves to the Joy of Cooking All About series.

My eternal appreciation goes to the food experts, writers, and editors whose contributions and collaborations are at the heart of Joy—especially Stephen Schmidt. He was to the 1997 edition what Chef Pierre Adrian was to Mom's final editions of Joy. Thank you one and all.

Ethan Becker

FOOD EXPERTS, WRITERS, AND EDITORS
Selma Abrams, Jody Adams, Samia Ahad, Bruce Aidells, Katherine Alford, Deirdre Allen, Pam Anderson, Elizabeth Andoh, Phillip Andres, Alice Arndt, John Ash, Nancy Baggett, Rick and Deann Bayless, Lee E. Benning, Rose Levy Beranbaum, Brigit Legere Binns, Jack Bishop, Carole Bloom, Arthur Boehm, Ed Brown, JeanMarie Brownson, Larry Catanzaro, Val Cipollone, Polly Clingerman, Elaine Corn, Bruce Cost, Amy Cotler, Brian Crawley, Gail Damerow, Linda Dann, Deirdre Davis, Jane Spencer Davis, Erica De Mane, Susan Derecskey, Abigail Johnson Dodge, Jim Dodge, Aurora Esther, Michele Fagerroos, Eva Forson, Margaret Fox, Betty Fussell, Mary Gilbert, Darra Goldstein, Elaine Gonzalez, Dorie Greenspan, Maria Guarnaschelli, Helen Gustafson, Pat Haley, Gordon Hamersley, Melissa Hamilton, Jessica Harris, Hallie Harron, Nao Hauser, William Hay, Larry Hayden, Kate Hays, Marcella Hazan, Tim Healea, Janie Hibler, Lee Hofstetter, Paula Hogan, Rosemary Howe, Mike Hughes, Jennifer Humphries, Dana Jacobi, Stephen Johnson, Lynne Rossetto Kasper, Denis Kelly, Fran Kennedy, Johanne Killeen and George Germon, Shirley King, Maya Klein, Diane M. Kochilas, Phyllis Kohn, Aglaia Kremezi, Mildred Kroll, Loni Kuhn, Corby Kummer, Virginia Lawrence, Jill Leigh, Karen Levin, Lori Longbotham, Susan Hermann Loomis, Emily Luchetti, Stephanie Lyness, Karen MacNeil, Deborah Madison, Linda Marino, Kathleen McAndrews, Alice Medrich, Anne Mendelson, Lisa Montenegro, Cindy Mushet, Marion Nestle, Toby Oksman, Joyce O'Neill, Suzen O'Rourke, Russ Parsons, Holly Pearson, James Peterson, Marina Petrakos, Mary Placek, Maricel Presilla, Marion K. Pruitt, Adam Rapoport, Mardee Haidin Regan, Peter Reinhart, Sarah Anne Reynolds, Madge Rosenberg, Nicole Routhier, Jon Rowley, Nancy Ross Ryan, Chris Schlesinger, Stephen Schmidt, Lisa Schumacher, Marie Simmons, Nina Simonds, A. Cort Sinnes, Sue Spitler, Marah Stets, Molly Stevens, Christopher Stoye, Susan Stuck, Sylvia Thompson, Jean and Pierre Troisgros, Jill Van Cleave, Patricia Wells, Laurie Wenk, Caroline Wheaton, Jasper White, Jonathan White, Marilyn Wilkenson, Carla Williams, Virginia Willis, John Willoughby, Deborah Winson, Lisa Yockelson.

Weldon Owen wishes to thank the following people for their generous assistance and support in producing this book: Desne Ahlers, Brynn Breuner, Ken DellaPenta, Arin Hailey, and Norman Kolpas. The photographers wish to thank Champ DeMar, San Francisco; Caruso/Woods, Santa Barbara; Beau Rivage, Santa Barbara; Nancy White; RubyLane.com; and Chrome Works.